For Harriet Bye and Frank Howard,
our partners in life as well as Tango.

Cover photo by Frank Howard
Cover models: Beatrice Satzinger and Michael Young
Cover design by Dale Moyer

Note for Librarians: A cataloguing record for this book is available from Library and Archives Canada at www.collectionscanada.ca/amicus/index-e.html
ISBN 1-4120-6413-9

Printed in Victoria, BC, Canada. Printed on paper with minimum 30% recycled fibre. Trafford's print shop runs on "green energy" from solar, wind and other environmentally-friendly power sources.

TRAFFORD
PUBLISHING™

Offices in Canada, USA, Ireland and UK
This book was published *on-demand* in cooperation with Trafford Publishing. On-demand publishing is a unique process and service of making a book available for retail sale to the public taking advantage of on-demand manufacturing and Internet marketing. On-demand publishing includes promotions, retail sales, manufacturing, order fulfilment, accounting and collecting royalties on behalf of the author.

Book sales for North America and international:
Trafford Publishing, 6E–2333 Government St.,
Victoria, BC v8t 4p4 CANADA
phone 250 383 6864 (toll-free 1 888 232 4444)
fax 250 383 6804; email to orders@trafford.com
Book sales in Europe:
Trafford Publishing (uk) Ltd., Enterprise House, Wistaston Road Business Centre,
Wistaston Road, Crewe, Cheshire cw2 7rp United Kingdom
phone 01270 251 396 (local rate 0845 230 9601)
facsimile 01270 254 983; orders.uk@trafford.com
Order online at:
trafford.com/05-1324
10 9 8 7 6 5 4

Acknowledgements

WE WOULD LIKE to thank Nora Dinzelbacher, Clay Nelson, Christina Johnson, Johanna Siegmann, Alejandro Oyuela and Nancy Mendoza for their suggestions after reading early drafts; Beatrice Satzinger and Michael Young for the cover pose; Dale Moyer for design assistance on the cover; Gayle Caldwell for editing the final manuscript; Walter Stillman and Raquel Mashiach for being photographic models; and to our wonderful Mendocino coast tango group that supports two nights of tango per week in a small community.

Table of Contents

Preface: What's So Tempting?

A BANDONEON WAILS. A spotlight swoops down onto the dashing and mustachioed man squeezing a moan out of the instrument draped over his knees, his head thrown back in closed-eyed concentration, perhaps ecstasy. The show begins. And so does our love affair with Argentine tango. It is 1995. The city is San Francisco. The show is "Forever Tango."

We wouldn't have our first lessons until 1999, something we still regret having postponed, but we would see "Forever Tango" twice more before our first lesson. What we witnessed at the show was stage-tango of course, called by some *Tango Fantasia*. As thrilling as it was to watch, that very thrill almost caused us to rule out tango for ourselves. How could we middle-aged dancers with merely adequate ballroom style pull off anything like *that*? Of course, what we didn't know about then is the tamer, unchoreographed Argentine tango danced by all kinds of people around the world, a form of tango which would have been accessible to us if only we had known how and where to begin.

Five years later, after many lessons and many miles traveled by our tango shoes, we're still blissfully addicted to our tango habit.

No one ever invokes the image of tango to describe the dull and sedate. When the word is uttered by non-dancers, their purpose is usually to conjure passion, whisk you into the exotic, push down on the accelerator. Even in TV commercials where its engaging sounds are meant to grab your attention and shift it to the product, the tango music itself always steals the show. Its volume and intentions are all over the board like a wild animal (or a sexy car). Even when slow, tango music is still lighting fires and probing. Do you care?—it seems to be asking. What do you want?

Tango to non-dancers is dominated by the dramatic; what they know of it are the flashy and fleshy exhibitions. Yet this is not the world that most dancers of tango know. Rather, it is a world of intimacy and sensuality combined with beauty and musicality—actually enough of all these to hold the tango dancer's attention through the arduous task of learning the dance.

In *The Temptation to Tango* we speak to both dancers and non-dancers. To the non-dancer we relate what it's like to tango. Not "how to," since this has been already attempted in writing with varying degrees of success. Our plan is to take you, our readers, through a vicarious tango embrace and show you the floor, the emotional banquet, the sensual feast. Then we'll hoist you onto our virtual shoulders for a literary trudge up the switch backs that led us to the garden of tango. To those who already dance it, perhaps our stories will resonate with your own experience and make greater sense of the difficult times we've all shared along the way. And remind you, too, why you fell in love with Argentine tango in the first place. Let's be clear right from the beginning that whenever we use the word "tango" we are referring to the Argentine variety, not to American or International Ballroom tango, which are the tango styles you may see in Ballroom competitions. The evolution of those styles from the original Argentine will be explained later in the section on tango history.

This book will show you how it happened to us and to others: what makes tango a musical art form, a romantic and sexual lure, a philosophy in movement, a cultural expression, a spiritual practice, an emotional release, or simply a form of exercise considerably more glamorous than what you'll find at your local gym.

Here, put simply, is *our* take on Argentine tango. We are both Americans, good friends, and frequent dance partners although our spouses remain our major dance partners. What may make our book unique is that it is from the points of view of two Americans taking on tango and sharing what we've learned about it, not tango authorities promoting a particular philosophy about learning it. The short stories are Larry's, the essays Irene's except where noted.

Together, these represent the multi-dimensional look at tango we think it deserves. Part fiction, part history, part philosophy, part journal, part romance, part how-to. Is it everything you need to know — or might want to know — about tango? Of course not. But in dance, as in life, one step leads to another.

Chapter 1

The Lure

IF YOU CAN conjure up at least a partial vision of what we're about to describe as the tango experience, you may fully grasp by the end of this chapter what we mean by tango's lure. Imagine this, to begin: A couple, strangers perhaps, walk into each other's arms at the first strains of the music. Subtly, almost imperceptively, they tenderly adjust their embrace for comfort and the purpose of lining up their bodies. Now intent upon the swelling surge of music, they open themselves to one another, almost breathing in unison, finding their connection as the music begins to move them. And move them it does. It might, in fact, be breaking their hearts. He shifts her weight to the intended foot, and she feels his intention to step out on the free one. Connected almost as one person in their upper bodies, they step out together on a strong beat of the music, and by the next step, they have created a kind of microcosmic world of their own. Nothing but the music and the two of them matter now. It's not possible, for the next three minutes, to think about jobs or shopping lists, or the headache one of them might have entered the room with. It's nothing but the tango now, fully absorbing, fully satisfying. Once a dancer experiences a "tango moment," that elusive moment when everything in the dancer's embrace seems to be in perfect balance and harmony, he may never be the same. Craving a repeat of the experience the way an addict craves a fix, dancers may spend a significant part of their lives seeking out the next tango moment. You'll meet some of these people in this book—some of them fictional, some of them real.

My husband, Frank, and I fall into the "real" category. It was real, all right, the way our pursuit of tango first took over our waking hours, then invaded our dreams, separately and together. We had never before had similar dreams and never expected to, being as different as we are. Yet there we were, both of us having dreams about dancing tango. We found this out one morning while lifting our heads from our pillows for the first conversation of the day.

"You had a tango dream, didn't you," Frank asked me. How can he tell?

"Look in the mirror," he says. When I do, what I see are sultry eyes, damp hair, flushed cheeks. All of them dead giveaways. Not to be outdone, but half jokingly, I point out his similar flush as I tweak his cheek.

"You had one too. That's how you know."

"If you tell me yours, I'll tell you mine."

What's going on here? Are we nuts? Maybe we are. Temporary insanity? Some non-dancing friends call us members of a "cult," but if tango is a cult, we don't seem to mind being brain-washed.

We often hear the music in our dreams, most likely whatever tango music we heard most recently, and to test this, we try humming it from memory. We see in our dreams beautiful dancing done by *los maestros* we might have seen recently on video or live in a class; then we feel ourselves mimicking their positions, their embrace, their footwork. With time, we progress as dancers in our dreams, in fact more progress than is evidently the case when we're awake. Which adds to our frustration. The damp faces upon awakening are not only from the physical effort held back by sleep, but from the frustration felt when the waking novice dancers must face the better dancers in our dreams. Will we ever get there, we wonder? Our fear, sometimes even expressed openly, is that we never will. And if there's any goal we share in common, it is to dance elegantly, skillfully, like any middle-aged Argentine couple who dance equally well with others as together. Our fevered responses, though, suggest there's much more to it. Some mysteries to plumb, some magic to either submit to or demythologize through regular practice. Might we eventually become bored by tango, once we are reasonably well-practiced and thereby privy to its secrets? We have yet to discover that possibility.

The Music

"Forever Tango" with its bandoneon-heavy orchestration, as it turned out, had tantalized primal memories out of me, memories of my father's accordion late at night as he punctuated the chords from that most famous of all tangos, *La Cumparsita.* (The bandoneon is a type of button accordion longer and narrower than most, with an exceptionally reedy and melancholy sound.) Of all the waltzes and polkas and pop music he played, it was this then-unknown-to-me tango title that I looked forward most to hearing. Even as a child I was aware of the pulsating tempo, staccato syncopations that set this piece off from the rest of his mitteleuropean and Middle American repertoire. Always a slow, deliberate, and part-time musician with a day job, he may have even been working on it when he died, I guessed, after looking again at the collection of sheet music he left me, which included a newer and updated version of *La Cumparsita.*

The first shivers of excitement I experienced, then, from Forever Tango's bandoneons and their opening glissandos were so primal in intensity, I've since often wondered if my father had played tangos to me in the nursery instead of lullabies. And the way my husband, Frank, gripped my hand, I knew he felt it too, either as a contact high from me, or from his own latent passion for this heartbreakingly dramatic and danceable music. That evening at the theater sparked a fever in us which has yet to be quenched. We would *not* be dancing American or International Ballroom style Tango again, that much was clear. And we're obviously not alone. In countries as various as Finland and Japan, large numbers of people are wild about Argentine tango and show no sign of being bored anytime soon.

There is no other partner dance we know of that allows you to dance out your feelings so freely—your fears, your delight, your response to the moment and to the music. And dancers agree, the music is the key. Listening to the music is what makes many people first want to tango. The drama of it, the rises and falls, surprising stops and pauses, alternating rubatos and staccatos, the long-fingered glissandos of piano or bandoneon and then the final almost orgiastic climb which signals the end is near. When it comes, you may find yourself breathing heavily, wiping your brow, and feeling like you've just performed something physical even though you've merely listened. It's not a passive experience, listening to tango.

Music critic, Bernard Holland, attempts to explain it:

> "The movement of tango music—originally two beats per measure, the first divided, and later 4/4 or 4/8 time—is seductive. So too are the harmonic progressions and repetitive song-form stanzas... Surrounding, indeed enveloping, is the dark beauty of the dance itself."

As your experience with the music grows, you inevitably guess that the vocabulary of dance steps must have evolved, to some degree, from responses to the music and the emotions it evokes. It is an intimate relationship that one can't help noticing, a bond between dancer and music that may be unique in dance history. Any tango teacher will tell you at your very first lesson to get a few CDs and listen to them in your car, with your breakfast, wherever you can get away with it. [See appendix 1, Tango Resources, for suggestions about music to seek out.]

Warning: tango, the music and the dance, may become addictive.

Brothels to Broadway... Tango History in Brief

Although there are a number of competing theories (and legends) about where tango comes from, and much argument about it to this day, there are a few things commentators agree upon about how the music and dance evolved almost simultaneously, and where the tango went from its original setting.

Like all tasty Latin American music, tango was created from spicy and diverse ingredients. Immigrants primarily from Spain, Italy, and Eastern Europe to Argentina in the late nineteenth century arrived

at the ports of Buenos Aires and Montevideo, where they met—and
some of them became—the shady types and petty criminals who
hung around in the back streets of *arrabales,* the *barrios.* There they
tossed their music and dances into a salad of existing folk music
and dances, dressed with the African drumming rhythms of the
candombe, and Cuban *habanera* brought by sailors. Some say the
new musical arrivals collided violently with indigenous musical
forms—as violent as were the knife fights among roaming men
competing for rare comforts in a foreign land—before any musical
fusion took place. Others claim that no recipe for collision or fusion
was ever intended. It just happened inexplicably, like other musical
hybrids of the New World, such as Afro-Cuban son and bolero styles.
But the result was an extraordinary creation, not a salad finally but
a stew simmered to an intense depth of flavor, a new music, not
unlike American Jazz in its evolution.

One Argentine musician and composer we know, Alejandro
Oyuela, stresses tango's African origins in the Kimbundu culture of
Angola as what made tango distinctive. The music of Angola, with
a rhythm unlike any other contemporary with it, made its first pass
to South America, he explains, through the Portuguese who had
colonized both Angola and Brazil, the latter a trader with Argentina.
When Alejandro played a recording of old Kimbundu music for
us, the rhythm was immediately recognizable as that underlying
the milonga rhythm we know today. (Here milonga refers to the
earliest style of tango, a style which is still danced in modified form
today. The word milonga also means a tango dance party.) Cuba, an
important hub to the slave trade, became a source of such African
rhythms through the Angolan slaves brought there for auction. By
the late nineteenth century the music of those slaves fused with
Spanish and French rhythms and resulted in what is known as
habanera, a popular form which Cuban sailors and travelers passing
through Cuba also carried to all ports of the New World, including
Buenos Aires.

Having come such a long distance, and without their women,
the immigrants' loneliness and hopeless longing shaped the arc and
poignant cry of this *criolla* (literally "Creole") music, perfect material

for the reedy wail of the bandoneon, an accordion-like instrument imported from Germany for the purpose of playing organ music during outdoor church processions. Not long for the religious world, though, it became the instrument of choice for tango music in clubs and bordellos, where it replaced the guitar and blended with other instruments to create a totally new sound. That sound fused musical qualities not usually combined: a strongly sentimental melody punctuated with abrupt rhythmic patterns and tempo changes. It was a freeing and stunning musical invention.

An emerging new social music incites new dances, and the tango embrace—alternatingly comforting, sensuous, dominating—defined the terms of the dance: heads and chests drawn closer together than in European embraced dances, thus allowing for the legs and feet to act out a physical drama of seduction and submission. It was probably the woman-hungry dock workers as they danced with each other in order to become skilled enough to compete for the tiny minority of available women, or to impress the most selective whores, who created the basic steps and adornments and principles of lead and follow.

Snubbed at first by the respectable upper classes of Buenos Aires, balked at for its lowly roots and rejected by serious culture vultures, tango music and dance styles were exported to a Europe deep in its fashion-conscious Belle Époque (early 1900's) and as so often with the outrageous and forbidden, the sensational and exotic, it was embraced by Europeans hungry for novelty—especially Parisians—as the latest, somewhat scandalous craze. Once it was condoned by Paris, Argentina's elite repatriated the tango and held it tightly, keeping at least several forms of it close to its original flavor, while both there and in Europe a cleaned-up version evolved, tame enough to be the subject of lessons, tea dances, and polite performances. By the 1930's, Carlos Gardel the Argentine singer-hero-saint, had become an international star, performing delicious tango "canciones," cabaret style, on stage and screen, and tango orchestras produced music with steady enough dance beats to fill the clubs with, at last, bourgeois Argentines.

According to Eduardo and Gloria, tango teachers with a great sense of humor and a solid knowledge of tango's history, salon dancers in the 1930's originally preferred to dance to recordings rather than to live music. This was because so many non-dancers went to the clubs to listen to tango orchestras that dancers complained the audience was too mixed, the passion diluted by different aims. But dancing to live music was certainly happening, our friend Alejandro insisted:

> "in the first two decades of the century small bands made their rounds through bars, restaurants and bordellos, to find venues with receptive audiences. They didn't play strictly tango but a mixture of indigenous folklore mixed with other European forms such as Spanish *pasodoble* and German *valses*. Tango was then an experimental form for musicians as well as dancers to explore."

Tango's golden age was 1920-1955, its heyday being the 1940's, when things dramatically improved for dancers. From 1935 on, the *orquesta tipica* of Juan D'Arienzo started playing for dancing, bringing dancers out again to fill dance halls and clubs. Tango singers were added, used as instruments, adding flavor and color and harmony. Other orchestras—their leaders both conductors and arrangers, sometimes composers, imitated D'Arienzo and then developed their own styles. It was the age of the D'Arienzo, DiSarli, and Troilo orchestras, to whose recordings from the 40's we still dance to today. We stared in disbelief, in fact, when our first tango teachers told us to buy only CD's of music made before 1945, but then found they were right to make that recommendation. At least for dance music... the steady beats of those orchestras, the lyricism and romanticism, nothing beats the music of the 40's.

A man had to be a good dancer to dance with a girl who danced well. If not, she'd never dance with him again, and to be rejected was cause for suicidal depressions, sometimes even acted on. "Dance first with the ten best dancers, "the advice would go, "then with anyone who would dance with you." Such advice was dependent, of course, on the skill of the dancer and how many women were present to choose from. Harkening back to tango's humble beginnings, when men danced with each other in back alleys and in bordello waiting-lines in order to better compete for partners in a then woman-scarce society, dancing skill turned out to be no less important to *tangueros* even in later decades' bigger ponds.

Teachers offered codes and patterns in print form, even teach-by-mail schemes. Naturally, there were academy dancing schools, some populated or staffed by faithful disciples of a particular teacher. In others there might be only partners to purchase: "you bought ten tickets to dance ten times at the milongas there," Eduardo explained to us in a workshop. "The best *tangueras* were the most sought after. A girl needn't be beautiful... even an ugly girl who can dance becomes beautiful." Meanwhile clubs of Buenos Aires were crowded every night with ordinary people of all ages dancing 'til they dropped, and returning the next night to do the same.

Many argue that it was the Beatles who killed off the tango in Argentina, the new rhythms of rock and roll bearing no relationship to tango and therefore displacing tango's young audience. The traditional *orquestas tipicas,* the big bands of tango, couldn't survive in this new atmosphere of imported new popular music.

But rock and roll was not the only enemy of tango. With the political troubles of the 60's, and the military repression and resulting curfews of the 70's, tango dancing either disappeared or went underground, sustained only through whispered memories, clandestine gatherings—as a window through which to view Argentina's mythic past. This was a past that included stoicism, the valor of the gaucho, the lonely cry of the immigrant, the violent undercurrent to street life—lying somewhere on the border between the urban and rural, and with a connection to a vital, if imaginary, moment in the nation's past.

Piazzolla and *Tango Nuevo*

The only newsworthy item about tango emerging from these dark days was the success of Astor Piazzolla's so called *tango nuevo.* New York-born and influenced by jazz, but musically raised in Buenos Aires and a star in Troilo's band of the 1940's, Piazzolla went to Paris in the 50's with the idea of becoming a modern composer. His mentor Nadia Boulanger proceeded to show him that his passion—and thus his future—lay in tango; of course it would be *his* tango, *tango nuevo*, as some of his admirers dubbed it. Piazzolla's compositions were indeed tangos. Not tangos, mind you, with steady beats and easy rhythms. These were tangos that were to the old tangos as bebop was to swing, not for dancing but for listening. Heady, loose, so variant that some compositions lend themselves to string quartets, others to jazz trios, a few even skirting rock and roll. And like the original tango *criolla*, *tango nuevo* enraged the middle classes and wasn't welcomed back in Buenos Aires until the 70's, after it had succeeded in Europe and the U.S.

In Carlos Suarez's Essay "El Jazz, the Tango," he highlights the parallels between *tango nuevo* and jazz.

> "We always sounded like distant brothers saluting each other and exchanging gossip! And like colonial brothers, we inherited a bit of that sense of inferiority instilled by our metropolitan colonizers... and the arrogant conservatism of our own people. Now Argentina resembles the music he prophetically composed long ago, when he was taking the modern but still conventional tango of the 1940's and 50's and developing it into his early pieces, laboriously dissembling the old tangos and rebuilding them in a modern form... into longer and larger compositions. Some of those longer works remind us of the evolution of Ellington in his older years, his concertos and oratorios." (from liner notes of *All them Cats in Recoleta,* a CD by *Tango No.9.*)

Tango the dance was not to reemerge for public and international appraisal until as late as 1985 with a film "The Exile of Gardel" followed by "Tango Bar" in 1987, and when a brilliant stage musical "Tango Argentino" showed up in New York in 1986 and started a renaissance of interest in both the dance and the music. To expat Argentines around the world, it was as if the Holy Grail had been returned to them. Their secret was out, and like tango's first diaspora at the turn of the century, this one too stirred pride in all things Argentine.

Smoke and Fire. Passion and Lust

The fact that tango evolved through an immigrant group's emotional expressions and as an antidote to their sorrow and sense of loss—sometimes attributed to their "exclusion" from bourgeois society—tends to give tango its haunting, longing qualities. What may have been happening throughout its evolution was a transformation of grief and sorrow into something of unimaginable beauty.

Tango's origins are about feeling, and even in its contemporary forms, whether on stage or in a dance club, it is a dance that's all about feeling. There is no other dance that allows you to dance out your feelings so originally, so intimately—your fears, your delight, your response to the moment and the music. And there's no denying that one of those feelings is sexual desire. Some argue that it was primarily sexual dominance that newly arrived men sought, and that the way the male lead evolved in tango displays that underlying urge toward dominance, even violence. Be that as it may (in Chapters two and three we will focus on the principles of lead and follow) the dance as a metaphor of sexual union necessarily underlies the lure of tango.

Stage tango is like tango on steroids (some say Viagra), with every move dedicated to the man-woman dance of sex: approach, flirtation, restrained passion, attempted seduction, resistance, reconsideration, rejection, reconsideration, conquest, climax, release. Accompanied of course by flash and sparkle and unlimited amounts of glamour. But even tango danced socially at a milonga reflects on a smaller scale the dance's preoccupation with sensuality. In the style called "close embrace" or club style, two bodies maintain full frontal contact at the chest with lower bodies slightly apart to allow for leg freedom. Even open style, salon style, which allows for a larger repertory of steps because partners hold a distance between them, inspires dancers to lay cheek against cheek whenever possible, with the man's hand cradling the woman's tenderly.

A milonga always looks and feels different from straight ballroom dances: the fragrance of men's cologne, the predominance of black silk, high heels even stilettos, fabrics that shine and stretch, just the right touches of glitter to make festive what otherwise sounds like heartbreakingly sad music. Women's earlobes drip long earrings, skirts either short and tight or long and slitted, both revealing considerable thigh. Women's pants are either skinny or wide—the young showing a bit of midriff, pleasing buns and trimly arched backs, older women elegant in wide legged palazzo pants, flowing and flattering. Even plumper women, and those who lead lives of predictable routine, in the arms of a skilled and generous leader can shape-shift into someone entirely different—"juicy tomatoes" I heard a man say to describe his partners, meant as a compliment of course.

The fact is, <u>all</u> women are beautiful when dancing tango. It's one of the rewards, the woman's progress from watching fantasy to making fantasy a reality. A *tanguera* becomes someone alluring, mysterious, and glamorous in a special way because she knows how to do something that lots of more beautiful women can't: she knows how to tango. Clay Nelson, of the Portland Tango Fest, adds this observation: "When you watch an accomplished follower dance tango, whether young, old, beautiful or not, she has not only learned how to move with her partner to the music, but she has also learned a highly stylized and flirtatious way of moving her feet, legs, arms and hands. It's really amazing and incredible to watch."

At ballroom dances, more often than not, there is a surfeit of single women. We have been to many milongas, however, where it's the men who outnumber the women. And some of these men are still beginners. Why, we wondered? How do they muster the nerve, my husband—who takes tango seriously—wonders. I could venture a guess: perhaps for a particular kind of man, tango dancing is too attractive to be resisted, its attractiveness canceling out residual shyness or an otherwise sensible modesty. Tango offers him such opportunity... to be masterful within a limited number of possible moves, to be in charge, to develop his own style in an already highly stylized atmosphere, to touch the hem of glamour and sensuality and move to fiery and passionate music... all without making a commitment longer than for the length of a dance. Of course, if he is polite or is acquainted with his partner he will—either from duty or from desire—dance at least the remainder of a *tanda* (the traditional 3 to 4 song set) with the same partner. Besides, American women at least are urged never to turn down an invitation to dance. And if a man is actively looking for something more than a temporary refuge in embrace, what better place to find a woman who wants to partner both ways?

Married couples trade dances regularly, with the understanding that dancing is just that, dancing, no matter how much the dancers enjoy the contact of the other's body. It is a legitimate and discrete sexual contact. Smooth fabrics in contact, beneath them smooth skin, firm flesh, supple muscles. Dancing improves muscle tone after all. The men who pull women close might give a sense of having gotten away with something, even under the gaze of their wives. No matter. The wives may also, sometime during this evening or next, be pulled close by someone else's husband.

Sharing our tango dreams as we do, my husband almost trembled when he told me about his dream of dancing with the lush Marcela in his arms the night after we'd had a lesson with them, Gavito and Marcela of "Forever Tango" fame. As teachers, they are known for the style that names their dual-persona: slow, sweet and hot. In Frank's dream Marcela leaned against the curve of his chest, ribcage against ribcage, he had felt her breath on his neck. I tried on a jealous response but decided not to buy it. Maybe if she had been someone attainable, I might have felt less generous. I'd like to think, though, that I've evolved beyond jealousy, that I'm becoming instead a *tanguera* whose understanding of tango-intimacy engenders confidence, not jealousy.

That same night, but earlier, we had heard lovers in the next room, making wheezy sounds during their lovemaking, imitations of the bandoneon, we ventured with a snicker. Tango music followed them even into bed. Do they have tango dreams too, we wondered?

Tango's Mysteries as a Lure Factor

Some students of tango insist there is a darker side to the passionate draw of the tango and to attending milongas. Juliet Taylor, an anthropologist/dancer who writes about tango history and tango psychology, describes it as both an addiction to pain and a relief from pain. The craving in the original populations, she says, was for "tango as relief from ordinariness or from loneliness or alienation.

Entering the tango club gave you the fix you needed—harmony, intimacy, ecstasy, belonging. You leave, it's over, you crave another fix." (Taylor, *Voz del Tango*: 6)

> In the same article, Taylor quotes a male dancer in Argentina today who has a strong opinion about why he's there at a milonga: "it's loneliness that leads dancers to the milonga. They can't form relationships because to surrender oneself is to face loss. Men go to the milonga to exert power. And in the milonga, power is in the hands of the man whom people can recognize as a Great Dancer. Women go to the milonga for consolation. But the milonga doesn't console; it only offers a moment of belonging. When they go out the door, men and women have nothing again and they leave with their pain. And that is the addiction. They must come back."

The mysteries behind the lure of tango are enough to spawn any number of theories. I happen to like this one based on "addiction." Even though the addiction my friends and I have known is not the desperate variety, the craving for relief from emotional pain, it still feels like an addiction. My husband and I feel something is wrong when some obstacle or other causes a week to go by without dancing in our living room. After the absence of tango for a week our bodies miss the unique comfort of the tango embrace, the slight lean toward one another that creates a kind of mutual support even though we are each supporting our own weight. We crave, yes I'll use the word, crave the moving in time to the music, the effects of a stylized and restrained passion that tango seems to emulate, the dancing of our feelings aroused by the music. We crave moving to the beat, around the beat, holding the beat long enough to embellish a step or start a complex figure that feels like a fugue in motion. Especially, we crave the pleasure of a step well-led and smoothly followed. The togetherness that tango requires. The permission to feel melancholy, express it with our bodies, revel in it, get some relief from it as from an orgasm, *"la petite morte"* as the French say. The magic of one body with four legs, as some call tango. Almost more than sex, it is an experience we have come to crave, and only tango fulfills the craving.

It's as if there was a magical place that most forms of transportation are unable to reach. Tango is one of the rare maps to this rarely discovered land where, once reached, the traveler can never again forget how glorious life can be; to leave this place is to be reminded of the mundaness of ordinary life (that is, life without tango). In the story to follow, you will meet a tango-enthusiast of a special order. For him, tango does a lot more than satisfy the senses; it fills a spiritual void.

"Immaculate Tango"

a story

FATHER GREGORIO HAD lived with the fear for eight years, expecting that one day someone else would know. But now, as the voice came to him from the other side of the confessional door, he was seized by a terror as if God had turned his face away.

"Father, forgive me, for I have been dancing intimately with a priest and have withheld the knowledge that I knew who he was." Father Gregorio's world froze and he knew no response. The silence seeped through the confessional cracks and turned into a poisonous gas. "Father, I'm not angry with you."

"I never meant to hurt anyone."

"You didn't, Father. I just can't keep it to myself anymore that I don't know who you are." She spoke fast now, afraid that the small door of opportunity might close. "I've avoided telling you ever since I knew for sure two years ago because I didn't want you to stop dancing. You tango beautifully, with such pleasure," her words slowed and softened. "It's not wrong, Father. I'm sure it's not. You should hear that from someone who knows and respects you. I want it to be a relief for you that I know."

"I have never lied to anyone about my dancing," was what he said, but he knew he had. He had never needed to lie directly because he had never been confronted about it. He had, though, side stepped many questions from dancers about "his work" and where he lived. Also, he made up the whole charade about an invalid uncle, allowing him an excuse to be gone for frequent days and evenings. In his mind, they had not been "false witness *against* thy neighbor," an important distinction in the context of breaking one of the Ten Commandments. However, this woman knew of his passion for tango and it would be forever different. "I just have never told anyone…because…"

"…because you're afraid people would think that a priest who tangos is doing something wrong…maybe even committing a sin. Believe me, I know how brutal people can be to public figures when they show weakness."

He wondered if her rushed whisper could be heard outside, though he hadn't noticed anyone waiting. Who was she? It wasn't proper to ask for her name in a confessional. Her voice sounded familiar, but he wasn't sure. He didn't know the women's voices for frequently they didn't even speak, as is common in tango. He knew their bodies, how they moved, and this is what brought him back to tango week after week. At first, he had deluded himself that it was the innocent love of the music that urged him to his first group class. Soon, though, he had to admit to himself that it was the parade of women through his arms that drew him like a religious conviction. Sure, he also felt physical desire, but he never lusted after them or pursued them for anything but another dance. In fact, he had cut short a growing attention from partners on at least two occasions. No, he had not broken his priestly vows; he had only learned to love women in the complete beauty of their spirit and earthly bodies, free from the sin and complications of sex. Tango had given him a way to love them that completed his life.

"Why did you decide to tell me here in the confessional?"

"Because here we can talk in private. On the dance floor it would be awkward and someone might overhear."

"I don't understand why you are telling me this unless you think it's wrong or too dangerous."

"What if I think it's right and I want to be there as a friend for you, if you ever need it?"

"I appreciate your offer of friendship, but the only way I can appropriately live these two realities is if they stay separate. Are you a member of this congregation?"

"No, I'm not really a member of any church, though I was raised Catholic. I live in Berkeley, which is why I know you from dances in the Bay Area. I've never seen you dancing at Sacramento events, not that I'm here that often."

"Dancing so close to home seemed too much of a risk." Had she come here to dance looking for him, he wondered? "How did you know that I was a priest?"

"You performed the wedding for a friend of mine, Jezebel White?"

"Yes, I remember."

"At first I couldn't place you, it's not like we had done anything more than dance a few times, but then the way you turned and took a step — suddenly I recognized you. I was tempted to tell my friends, but I thought right then it was best kept secret. Two weeks later, when we danced at the Broadway club, dancing with you reminded me of a holy sacrament." Father Gregorio felt danger from being in the trajectory of a loaded phrase and his chest tightened. "Please don't think I'm making fun of you," she went on, "I mean this with all sincerity. To be the holder of this secret enriches me every time we dance. I told myself that I was coming here today as a support to you, but I feel so relieved, I see that it was really for me. It didn't feel right to know who you were and not to tell you."

"This will make it difficult for me to dance with you."

"Why Father? I'm not going to dance differently with you than I have before. The affectionate way you dance with me and the others...? That can't be wrong in the eyes of God."

"It's not God I'm worried about."

"No one else will find out from me, I promise." A long silence stretched between them. Father Gregorio searched for words as the light poured in through the breach in the wall of his guarded inner life. It might anger her, or worse, hurt her to ask that she never dance with him again. "Father, I need to go now. Please don't stop dancing," her voice hung like the tone of a bell between rings, "and trust me for another tango?"

What more was there to say in this conversation he never wanted to have? "All right. Thank you for keeping this knowledge to yourself." And she was gone. He caught a slight glimpse of her through the filtered window, but not enough to know for sure who she was. It could have been worse, a lot worse. Yet, she must want something, he thought, or she wouldn't have told him at all. The membrane between the Church and the tango was bleeding back and forth a blood which was never meant to be mixed. The confessional door opened and shut and another voice confronted him.

"Father, I've sinned with my boyfriend. I didn't think that we would go that far. I'm not pregnant, but now he wants me again…" Father Gregorio, for the moment, was back inside the familiar world of the Church.

Father Gregorio removed his priestly vestments and sat down in front of the mirror. How much smaller he always looked to himself without his robe. He ran his hand through his black hair, now half gray and saw vertical lines in his cheeks that he didn't remember. Did she think he was handsome, he wondered? It will be easier if that isn't the case. He thought it remarkable that it had taken this long to be found out. Not that he hadn't been exceedingly careful. When first learning to tango, he had switched from group classes to private lessons early on to minimize his chances of being recognized. Yet it was during the group classes at a small number of tango conventions, located far from California, which had provided some of the highlights of his life. In the relaxed nature of a class where partners rotate, there isn't the drama of searching out and asking a partner, only women willing to be held and moved.

At least the Catholic Church approved of dancing; had he been a Protestant Minister of the many Christian sects that he knew of, dancing wouldn't be tolerated at all. At least then the opportunity for discovery by a devout parishioner would be reduced to something similar to a first hand experience of the Second Coming. He smiled at himself in the mirror realizing that if he were a minister of almost any other religion, he would be married as well. Perhaps then he could have sex, but not tango. Strangely, this seemed less natural to him than his own predicament. For it wasn't the fulfillment of sexual desire that he missed the most from his solitary calling. What he ached for was an intimate bonding of another kind, a visceral connection with a female body that happened deeper through the hands and chest than even a sexual embrace—or so he assumed.

The one sexual relationship he had had before the priesthood had left him feeling drained and off balance with his partner. From the inferences during counseling sessions, he knew that sex was less than satisfying for one or both partners a good deal of the time. But what he felt holding women close in a tango was something purer, even holy and it suffocated his heart to think of giving it up.

What would the Church think, if they knew? Would they suspect that his relations with women weren't confined to the dance floor? How could he ever explain himself to the congregation or other priests? Maybe it wouldn't be as bad as he feared. No, it would be. Priests don't dance with women for hours at every opportunity, especially the most intimate and passionate dance of all. If the wrong person knew, he would have to choose, assuming the diocese didn't choose for him. Up until now, he had always thought that he would choose the Church and priesthood—there seemed no question.

Since the day of his exposure in the confessional, he let the week slip by without attempting to attend a milonga. The next week, too, he didn't dance, not wanting to confront his fears. The following week was his Sunday off in the rotation, the easiest week for him to attend the bigger weekend dances. He resolved to dance again, realizing now that his greatest fear was facing the woman who knew him, though her identity was still a mystery. He had considered flying to Los Angeles, it was quick and cheap enough. It wouldn't be a pattern he could sustain though. No, better to go to a Bay Area dance and trust his confidante. The once a month all night milonga was this Saturday in Berkeley; he might as well take advantage of it.

The space of the Berkeley milonga was void of the charm of San Francisco's Broadway club with its balconies of dark wood and red curtains. Nevertheless, he had received some of his richest gifts on this dance floor. It reminded him of his own church, a large modern rectangle lacking the character of hundreds of cathedrals he had visited in America and Europe. Somehow though, the Spirit could still flourish in such surroundings; it dwelled in the living temples that stepped to the ecstatic and demanding rhythms of the tango.

Father Gregorio arrived after eleven, hung up his coat, and entered

the sanctuary. He wore his usual turtleneck long-sleeved shirt, black
this time; the high neck was a comfortable reminder of his normal
collar, but meant nothing to anyone else. His slacks were off-white.
Before him were a hundred places of worship, extending their legs
behind them into the unseen line of dance. Several also stood by the
walls or sat in chairs like altars. Which one was she? Was she here at
all? He recognized several women that he had danced with before,
but he could only know her through her voice and the telltale look
of knowledge in her eyes. She would have to let herself be known.

He asked Rebecca to dance, a woman who had been a friend for
a long time, knowing that they always had a fine rapport. Resting
their chests gently together, they found the familiar connection of
arms and hands — consistent with the conventions of the tango, but
yet so specific to each partner that he would recognize them with
his eyes closed. Rebecca wrapped her left arm as high across his
neck as she could reach and held on tight, making some maneuvers
difficult. Some partners love to be whisked through a series of
quick flashy moves, but Rebecca only wanted to be held close and
guided through tango walks and close turns. She never verbalized
this desire — she didn't have to — the way she attached herself left
no option; leaders that were uncomfortable with her preference
simply didn't ask her to dance again. Father Gregorio had never had
more than perfunctory conversation with Rebecca, though they had
danced together on well over fifty nights. He didn't even remember
anymore whether she was a doctor or a typist and guessed that his
inarticulate descriptions of his own career had long slipped her
recollections. What they knew of each other was the celebration of
the ineffable mystery of opposites and the necessity to be held by
another human being.

Father Gregorio never danced only one dance with a partner, unless
she declined the offer of another. If the first dance had not gone well,
a second and third would be required to discover a new connection
and learn how he needed to expand his abilities to encompass this
new embodiment of human potential. If the first dance had been
pleasurable, to quit after one would be a sacrilege to the union of
tango. Somewhere between three and five songs was the appropriate

duration of devotion to each partner; more than five songs might be misconstrued and be difficult to back away from.

After Rebecca, he chose Sarah. Sarah preferred more physical distance than Rebecca, but not out of shyness to the embrace of a man. She wanted to be seen and kept her eyes on him far more than anyone else he danced with. When he met her eyes and smiled softly, he could feel her heavy bearing on his upper arm lighten and a buoyancy from acceptance renew her steps. He was sure she wasn't overtly conscious of this herself, but he experienced this same progression with her nearly every time and delighted in ministering to her self-esteem. By the third and fourth dances she had softened and relaxed her chest to nuzzle lightly against him, though taking distance in turns to make eye contact again.

Next, he noticed Lonnie, who had been one of the women who had sought more than friendship. He had avoided her for a while, until she had become serious with another man. Then it was safe to dance again and they renewed their love of tangoing together. She was a feather in his arms, sometimes an elusive mouse, changing positions and holds while they danced and talking more than anyone, for most didn't talk at all while dancing. She would narrate the progress of the dance and weave it into the current state of her own well being. At first, this had annoyed him, but then he felt the rhythm of her ramble and saw how it mirrored their dancing and that he could direct her flow of commentary instantly with gentle squeezes and vivid gestures to enunciate a step. She wasn't thinking through the conversation, it was just a part of her expressiveness. He fancied that she gained steadiness from him and he sought to be a place of comfort for her. Lonnie always gave him a solid hug at the end of a dance set together and accompanied it with an affectionate sisterly kiss on the cheek. As she walked away, Father Gregorio thought that he couldn't have been a better example of priesthood than the way he had been with Lonnie.

It was deep into the night now; the hour having long since past when a neighbor seeing your return would not wonder at the occupation which had kept you until this rare and challenging stretch of the darkness. Regular modern dance clubs were about to close and men and women were clumsily pairing off with strangers, barely able to scream over the din of loud music and without a dance form to introduce and guide them through the perilous intricacies of union. On his way to the drinking fountain in the hallway, Father Gregorio was stopped by a hand on his arm and a familiar voice. "I'm very happy to see you dancing again. I hadn't seen you anywhere the last couple of weeks and was hoping that I hadn't done the wrong thing."

The timbre of the voice from the confessional was unmistakable. "This is the first time I've had a chance. Though, I'll admit, I've been very anxious since we talked."

"Anxious that I want something from you that you can't give?"

"Or that you want me to be both parts of my life at the same time, which isn't allowed. I almost asked you to dance a little earlier tonight, not knowing that it was you who came to me."

She grabbed his arm and pulled him down an empty hallway out of earshot. "You didn't know!"

"I couldn't see your face and I wasn't sure by your voice. And you never said your name."

"Why didn't you ask?"

The question caught him off guard. "I have avoided asking questions of my dance partners all along, partly to discourage having to answer them myself."

"But my name…you already knew that."

"Knowing who you are with so much revealed between us is very different."

Her eyes were wide and she closed nervous lips. The same weight that pulled the corners of her mouth to a frown began to weigh her whole face down. Father Gregorio wondered if there were words she wasn't allowing herself to say. "Will you dance with me now? he asked."

Her eyes raised by themselves, as if they alone couldn't overcome the burden that now held her. Slowly the question sunk in. "Yes."

He led her by the hand to the dance floor and brought her slowly close to him. For now, she had taken on the fear for both of them and Father Gregorio again felt strong. They started to dance with a few inches between them, but it was awkward; they had always danced touching before. He pulled against her back and brought her feminine chest to settle against his. She leaned her forehead against his neck. It had not been the beginning of a song when they started and it ended soon after they entered the floor. He kept her in the close embrace until the next tango started and they began again.

She waited for every step he would lead. All turns were slow. He only wanted to stay in rhythm with his arms around her. They spoke not a word between songs, nor did they allow physical space to creep between them. With his mind's eye he imagined her feet as he placed her step by step. He would make contact with her feet frequently, in tango form, letting her know that he knew where she was. And more importantly, he let himself be known to her. In the early hours of morning on a crowded floor, the two of them could know the unspeakable, held and protected by music and dance.

He lost count of the dances. She gave no indication of wanting to leave. Words had no use. The music was the life sustaining breath of their intimacy and the physical craft of the dance was their private shelter. They roamed a lifetime of possibility on a thirty by forty-foot wood floor, part of a greater congregation worshiping the mystery of two bodies together. Adherence to the subtly complicated form of the dance was to honor your partner, and in so doing, give you a glimpse at the divine.

Tango had become something sacred, set apart from other worldly pursuits much in the same way as his priesthood. Father Gregorio spent a great deal of his life in active prayer, acknowledging and beseeching his chosen figure of God for connection and guidance. In a similar way, he yearned for a language of words to have tango make some sense. As he danced now with this woman who knew him, he felt a need for words. They had danced dangerously long, obscuring the protocol for finishing their stay in each other's arms. He knew it would have to be over soon, but it couldn't end like all the others. They had gone too far to pretend that theirs was an ordinary dance. Something had been conceived between them. It was beautiful and it was yet unnamed. Opportunities presented themselves at the end of every song—a build-up, a last beat, and with that, a pose that represented completion. He returned her weight to both feet, squeezed her tightly for a few seconds, and quickly led her to an unoccupied corner of the room. Standing next to chairs piled with coats required for the cold air outside, he held her shoulders with both hands and spoke to the woman only a few inches away.

"Thank you, Maria. I hardly know what to say, except that I have never felt better in my life than I just did dancing with you." Maria said nothing, but her eyes were pools of contained water and her mouth trembled. "You have given me a gift that is probably greater than I should have, but I am deeply grateful. I think I had best leave now."

"No. You should dance with someone else right now, someone besides me. One more dance and then you can go."

"Why would I want to dance with anyone else after what we just had?"

"Trust me. Please. I'm going to leave now, but you need to dance one more time tonight. Tell me that you'll dance with me again soon and I'll be very happy."

He did. She kissed his cheek hard, said "Thank you for a wonderful dance, Peter" and left. He stood facing the door she exited aware of her tear that had baptized his cheek. He wiped it softly and looked at his hand. Slowly he turned around and looked again at the crowd of dancers who seemed wholly unaware of the drama that was his. He felt so like a virgin compared to those who moved past him and thought that this was probably a proper way for a priest to feel. Not far from him a woman stood alone looking with what he guessed to be longing towards the dance floor. He walked over and asked her to dance, receiving a broad smile and her hand.

They had never danced before and he searched for how she could fit in a tango hold. He was amazed at how unfamiliar she felt, even though her body was not so radically different from Maria's. She was an experienced dancer though and soon they flowed into the sea of partners. He felt steadied again and wondered if this was why Maria had told him to dance once more with someone else. Or was it so that she could leave first and alone? Had she wanted him to say something else?

He was aware of the darkness of the room now in the most silent part of the night. Several recessed lights were turned down to a soft glow. In the middle of the room was a simple modern chandelier that glowed stronger than the other luminaries. He found himself drifting to the center of the room under the brightest light.

The Power of Exoticism and the Dark Side of Tango

Even the sedate costume dramas of BBC's Masterpiece Theater have been marked by tango. Their 2002 production of "The Forsyte Saga" includes a speech from a character recently returned from Buenos Aires circa 1902, his hoarse whisper a mixture of confidentiality and shock: "There's this dance they do in Buenos Aires. It's exciting beyond words when you first see it... but it's a dreadful thing. Men and women clutching together, it's as if what isn't meant to be seen *is* being seen ... in the streets. There's evil in it."

I was startled at the intensity of this character's disapproval, especially as it is presented as one of the reasons for which this gregarious gambler and ladies' man left Argentina to return to his family in England. But "Evil in it?" For the first time, listening to these words, I palpably felt the force of all those accounts I'd read about tango's shock value to polite society. By today's standards of course, hardly evil. Exotic, however, is another matter.

Tango is often called exotic, its many commentators attributing tango's popularity in fact to the perception of it — since it first was seen outside the *barrios* — as exotic. But what does this word actually mean in the tango context? And why is exoticism such a draw?

It helps to understand the power of tango as an exotic import when one considers the milieu of the pre-war Europe it was brought to. At the turn of the century, also known as *la Belle Époque,* ballroom and social dancing were in full swing as a pastime, both the rowdy folk versions of the working classes and the more sedate waltzes of the leisure classes, which had themselves evolved from rustic country waltzes and contra dances. In cities, social dancing was clearly becoming differentiated from the spectacle of dancing entertainment on the stage. Still, the more scandalizing stage dances primed the scene to some degree for equally scandalizing social dancing. Onto the Montmartre cabaret stages came the French can-can and Apache dancing, followed by imports such as belly dance, flamenco, and finally, tango.

Onto the dance floors of dance halls and salons came the dances that Marta E. Savigliano, a noted dance scholar calls "colonized exotics," the dances like tango and the African cake walk which drew forth moral disapproval in some quarters but were eventually expropriated and exploited by the elites, tamed and minced into a form just naughty enough to be nice. Irresistibly fascinating. Exotic. Exotic because they were foreign by virtue of class origin or ethnic origin, exotic because they impelled feelings of superiority mixed with curiosity and titillation. There would be, both in Europe and in Argentina, an evolution in tango from what Savigliano calls "away from ruffianism and toward romanticism," but for some period both extremes existed simultaneously. Learning to dance tango was akin to what was happening nearly at the same time in New York: whites going uptown to Harlem to listen to ragtime and early swing, and later to do the Lindy Hop and jitterbug.

Savigliano strives to explain some of the complexity that surrounded the thrust of tango onto to the European scene. She first fits tango into the broad category of anti-bourgeois, and anti capitalist rebellions during the Romantic era which just preceded its arrival. The search for exoticism in Europe was fed in various degrees by exotic imports to many of the decorative arts; consider for example the influence of chinoiserie, japonica, Gaugin's natives, Africa's primitive masks, and Egyptiana. In the world of social dance, this same European hunger for exoticism seemed to have paved the way for the tango as an import, but it was not a simple matter of connecting the dots or a simple set of circumstances.

> "...the tango, a hybrid in terms of race and class in its original setting, generated mixed feeling of acceptance and rejection at both extremes of the Parisian class structure. The mixed reactions at multiple class levels were signs of the simultaneous operation of class, race, and nationality markers in European society, markers that contradicted each other when facing exotics. The reactions to tango were showcases of these complex social tensions. In the early 20th century, tango brought novelty in the exotic genre—a distinguished and demimonde, urbane exoticism from the already independent colonial world. Tango was an exotic genre suited to the complex modern imperial bourgeois ordering of the world ...it was a perfect candidate for the modern capitalist condition. The tango was originally poor but moving upwards,

urbane with some traces of ruralness, white with some
traces of color." (Savigliano: 110)

If capitalist exhaustion needs periodic renewal, what better tonic
than tango?

Unlike other exotic performed dances such as French can-can
and belly dancing and other Orientalist dancing, stage tango did
not focus on the female body alone, but rather on the process of
seduction... a *femme fatale* who revealed her passions but ultimately
kept them under control. Admitting female sexuality, remember,
was a relatively new thing. Across the channel it was known as the
Victorian era. But in Paris, the display of equal sexual tension between
man and woman, and shared equally in a dance of intertwined legs,
was making a debut in the form of tango, and it must have been an
astonishingly arousing experience for the viewer. Also fascinating
was the enigma behind the apparent, but still subtle, ambiguity of
the sensual woman seeming to need male protection to serve as
a support for the pent up eroticism present in them both. Heady
stuff, and certainly original to everyone but the most bohemian of
Parisians.

Business promotion being foremost in the minds of at least some
bourgeois observers, it wasn't long before dance masters came forward
with their anesthetized, simplified, codified versions that could be
taught to adventurous ladies and gentlemen. Not far behind were
the spectacle impresarios and the fashion designers, with their ideas
for dancing slippers, split skirts and faux Latin accessories. The split,
then, between performed tango and danced tango became irrevocable.
Music hall stage tango became more and more stylized and complex
and athletic, while European tango dancing by couples in ballrooms
became Internationalized, codified—and with the influence of the
British ballroom movement—snapped neatly into something that
bore little relationship to the original fiery tango. Just watch a tango
danced in an International ballroom competition to get an accurate
picture of how dances can evolve—or devolve—through social and
economic manipulation.

On this side of the Atlantic, it was Rudolf Valentino's interpretation
of the tango in "The Horsemen of the Apocalypse" which provided
the impetus for an emerging American-style ballroom tango. Easy to

parody for its stiff imitation of passion enflamed by a rose between the lips, it too has acquired place in competitions and bears little resemblance to the real thing.

This promoting of tango led, in fact, to so many different styles that even back at home in Argentina, the middle and upper classes "demanded refined styles, not only different from the style of the rough ruffians but also distinguishable from the exoticized versions developed in Paris, London and New York." (Savigliano: 149) Tango, it seems, was also to be the victim of a need for class and national identity, the result being that off and on since the 20's, there has been among old *tangueros* and young scholars a search for both tango's true origins and an authentic "pure" tango.

What was diluted by promoters—while insisted upon by purists—were the dark origins of the tango. Purists believed a popularization movement threatened "to wash out the dark origins of the tango—origins of exploited people—and silence the history of race-class-colonial confrontation that had contributed to tango's multiple hybrid cultural expression." Savigliano explains that *tangueros* who had known the old tango perceived this popularization on stage as tango's death, its more complex underpinnings of conflicts in "race, class, and imperialist tensions," now usurped by the more universal act of sexual tension.

While tango's origin was richly steeped in the spirit of a rebellious counter culture, a musical street culture defying not only bourgeois behavior but the exploitation of immigrant workers, tango was being shifted to the entertainment arena. Rather than dancing out the larger social, racial, and imperialist conflicts that were of political interest to some social historians preoccupied with colonialism, tango was now regarded to be primarily about sex, and that's where it was to stay. The restraint of passion, both implicit and explicit in tango's form, which Savigliano and others believe originates from non-sexual, socio-economic sources, came to be perceived of in terms of erotic gender conflict alone.

In response to this shift, Savigliano, the choreo-critic, opines:

> "The scandalous colonial, racial, and classist histories of tango had been pacified under the exaggeration of its erotic display. In tangos, gender and heterosexuality had been regarded, so to speak, as the main contradiction, but this complex history was endangered by tango's

popularization and diversification, each of which encouraged forgetfulness." (Savigliano: 156)

Those of us who love tango tend to willingly suspend—or forget—the more painful parts of tango history for the sheer pleasure of the dance. Some of us—especially when we hear the *maestros* talk about tango as an expression of Argentina's national sufferings—feel a tinge of guilt for our pleasures. But mostly, for our purposes, here among the tango diaspora in the 21st. century, at a time when ballroom dancing of all kinds has enjoyed a revival of interest, we are infinitely grateful that some equally enterprising Argentineans in the late 1980's revived an interest in a *Tango Argentino* far closer to the original than what we had been offered in ballroom studios, a tango (or more accurately a group of tango styles) once again danced nightly in the clubs of Buenos Aires and in clubs, dance studios, ballrooms and festivals in this country as well as others.

Not long ago we were shown a video production in progress about elderly *tangueros* of Buenos Aires. "Chasing the Ghost" it is titled. In it we see and hear the "old ones" attesting to the role of tango in their lives: tango IS life, more than one of them claims. Dancing the tango is like cheating death, they imply. It is passion personified, one can live FOR tango; all the yearnings, longings that are implicit in being human are acted out in tango. The film ends with a scene in a hospital, interviewing an elderly tanguero, the recent victim of a heart attack. To his doctor he says with complete certainty and a total absence of irony: "If I can't tango any longer, pull the plug."

Even though elderly *porteños* (residents of the port of Buenos Aires) claim that you have to be at least 50 to understand tango lyrics, one can still be permanently changed by encountering tango at a young age. The young American in the next story had tried many different antidotes to his *ennui,* but it would be tango, discovered accidentally, that would fill his life as nothing else had.

Just Ten Steps

a story

SABRINA'S GARDENIA-SCENTED wrist stroked against Jared's cheek on her way to enveloping him, almond oil and sweat like a fine mist of ocean spray mixing with the tropical flower and carrying him to a mythical island. He ached to run his hands along her naked back; instead, they lay contained at his side on the couch according to the rules of the Golden Room Gentleman's Club, squeezing her feet and ankles when they came within reach.

A pop song of electronic innovation pounded to completion while another pounced on its tail and continued the chase. "That makes six songs Jared. Shall I keep going?" Sabrina asked, cradled naked in his lap. Her breath blew across his ear.

"Two more, sweetheart. You don't need to do much."

Straddling his legs while sitting on them, Sabrina opened the top two buttons of his shirt, wrapped her arms around his neck, and pressed her breasts against the skin of his chest. She laid her cheek on his and did nothing for the first song except kiss and nibble his ear. During the second song, she opened his legs and slipped her belly and hips between them and rested her lower belly against his crotch. Still hugging his neck and pressing her forehead into his, she twisted her naked middle into him.

The song ended. "Are you sure you don't want one more?"

"I want the whole night with you."

"That's not one of the options, Jared."

"I'd make it very worth your while."

"Do you have any idea how many offers like yours I get every week?"

"You never accept any of them?"

Sabrina uncoiled from Jared's lap and sat beside him. "I did once and I never will again." She suddenly looked very small. Gone was the welcoming and cocky smile. "I'm sure you'd be different, but…"

"It's all right," Jared didn't let her finish her sentence. He paid her for the eight dances, the second round he had had with her that night, also the second time he had come to the club to be with her that week.

When she was clothed again in her lingerie, she gave his hand a brief squeeze and offered, "Don't take it personal."

Outside the Gentleman's Club was asphalt and engines. Jared felt the shock of the harsh surfaces and zipped against the cool autumn air. He walked the hundred feet to his silver Toyota Rav 4 and leaned on the back door. Taking a deep breath, he imagined his hands on Sabrina. Had she said yes to his offer he would no doubt have had to exceed his monthly stipend in only the middle of the third week. He could afford to spend another hundred, maybe. He shifted his weight off of his car and took a step back towards the club and stopped. A few more minutes with Sabrina and then what? The same place he was now minus a hundred dollars. Jared stood motionless in the parking lot, caught in a self-imposed gridlock.

Two men arrived and walked past this thirty-eight year old man, giving him no more notice than most people did. Jared was only five-foot-six, slender, with narrow eyes and the fine nose and cheeks of his mother. Somewhere in Eastern Florida his nervous little mother, Diana, was attempting to quit smoking after her diagnosis of emphysema last month. Twelve years ago, shortly after she had turned fifty, Jared's father, Floyd, had left her for a Hawaiian model in her thirties that he met while overseeing the construction of a new sports center in Honolulu. Now his father lived on the beach in Maui with his native wife and three young daughters whom Jared had only seen four times in ten years.

For the past two years, Jared had maintained himself in a small apartment in San Francisco, seeing his mother once a year on Thanksgiving. He hadn't spent a Christmas with his family since his last year in college, the year that Diana erupted in a flow of scathing insults towards her husband on Christmas morning. Two weeks earlier a friend had reported to Diana that she had seen Floyd entering a hotel room with a young woman she didn't know. Jared's mother had decided to unwrap all the surprises at once while everyone was gathered around the tree. Instead of reminiscing most memorable Christmases with the next of kin, Jared now preferred to seek parties with single women to share a chorus or two of holiday cheer. Ski lodges, resorts, bars and lounges, all contained lonely women on Christmas Eve. Meanwhile, the five thousand a month from his grandfather's trust fund arrived in his account the first of every month as it had for the last fourteen years.

Jared left his car and bolted down the sidewalk of North Beach. Something felt like it was trying to crawl up out of his belly and he had learned to choose a fast walk rather than the cigarettes of his mother. How frequently he had wished that he had inherited the physical features of his father, his height, his broad handsome face, and, maybe more than anything, his ability to be first in line and take two pieces of the pie, never counting how many people were present.

Posters of outrageously sexy women promised him satisfaction inside club after club. Real women with tired come-ons stood at the doorways and beckoned him to ache for what he couldn't have. At least he had received his father's sexual drive, though it seemed a cruel joke on one as plain as him. He knew of a prostitute he could call and feed the python that prowled silently in his inner jungle; an hour with Michaela and the snake would coil in repose for another few days. Michaela would mean poverty rations of bread and cheese for a week. He stopped into a pizza joint and ordered a Hawaiian Special of pineapple and ham. Chewing on the oily mass he realized that he was eating bread and cheese anyway and decided to call Michaela.

He hit the street again on the way to his Rav 4 and cell phone. Coming towards him were three women walking together that were so beautiful he stopped so as to lengthen the time he could trace the outline of their curves. He guessed that they worked at one of the clubs and were either coming or going. A few feet before him they turned left and entered a doorway he wasn't familiar with. Closing the distance to where they had disappeared, he saw them for a moment as they ascended a long stairway, their excited voices cascading back down to dance on his shoulders. Entering a few steps, the clatter of traffic sounds were replaced by a music he didn't know. What was this place? What was the cost? Was it a private party?

Jared climbed the steps up to a woman at a desk and peered into the room. People were dancing to a music of heartbeat pace and leaning into each other.

"The entry fee is ten dollars," said the woman at the desk.

"What is this?"

"Tango. Take a look and if you want to stay come back out and pay me."

Jared ducked his head inside. Most of the room was a dance floor with a ring of tables around the outside. The floor and sides were packed and everywhere he looked were stunning women. They weren't all young like the sex clubs, but such grace they had. He paid the maitre-di the nominal entry-fee and walked over by the bar on the far side.

Jared took a seat, but didn't lean back. In front of him bare calves stretched, flared, fanned, and kicked softly before lengthening for the next back step, her skirt stretching to mid-thigh, muscles becoming firm, then relaxed. The next woman had her arm wrapped high around the man's neck, her blouse inching up her belly; a deep lean against her partner exposed all the way to her first ribs. One after the other they paraded past, seemingly oblivious to the affect they were having on him. One woman opened her eyes and met his for a brief moment, only to close them again as if rolling over in her sleep. Judging from the soft upper curve of her mouth, her dreams were rich.

Jared noticed other things. After a few dances, nearly everyone changed partners. He had assumed from their chest to chest abandon and interlaced arms and legs that most of the dancers were couples. He overheard one couple exchange first names after they had danced. They had just met! And then the most striking thing of all, he saw that during every dance there were at least fifteen women

not dancing, standing or sitting at the edge of the floor while maybe
five men watched or chatted by the bar. He took a moment to check
out the men dancing. They too were of all ages, sizes, and shapes
and with rare exception, the women in their arms were beautiful.
How could this be?

Jared ordered tequila at the bar and approached a man standing
alone by the floor. He guessed him to be about fifty with a small gray
goatee, dress pants and a black tee shirt. "Is this hard to do?"

"What? The tango? Yeah, deceptively so." He sprouted a wide grin.
"Not as hard as living with my first wife was."

"How do you learn it?

"Oh god, there are classes all over the place nearly every night.
Then, after a few weeks, take some private lessons."

"That's it?"

The goateed acquaintance gave an airy snort and replied, "That
and many months, then years, and giving up a lot of whatever else
you've been doing."

Depending who asked, Jared could be doing a lot or very little. He
had stuck it out for a degree in Art History, though what he had
enjoyed the most were the few creative classes he had taken. His
parents had always assumed that he would continue in graduate
school in a more employable discipline, but he had only gone to
college in the first place because of the ample financial support. He
stretched a four-year degree into six, changing majors twice. His
grandfather died soon after he graduated, his grandmother already
dead. Five thousand a month isn't riches, but Jared didn't have to
earn money. Neither did his father have to work after that point, but
his father's work was a source of his power.

Jared spread out the tango class advertisements on his kitchen
table that he had collected in the lobby of the dance hall. Most of the
flyers had a picture of the teachers; all of their faces, if not beautiful,
were captivating. He recognized two of them from the dance that
evening. Looking up he saw his half-finished clay sculpture of a
naked woman arching her back. Her breasts, belly, and hips near
completion, but the head and legs a mess. Of course, this was all right

in art; they didn't have to be finished for the work to be complete. Was this tango dance something he could get? He had never done anything more than bounce around to rock-and-roll, when he was drunk enough. Maybe tango would be something else that he would start and not finish; though he wondered how one could ever tell with a dance that it was complete.

His message machine was blinking. "Jared, this is Mom." Her voice was shaky. "We haven't talked in a while…How are you? My test results weren't good. Give me a call when you can." Jared stared numbly at the machine. "Jared, Dad here. How are the sculptures coming? Let me know if you've got a show. Simpson still says he could set you up in a management position at the arena if you want it, but don't wait forever. So spend some of your granddad's money on a call sometime." What a night this was, calls from both parents and stumbling upon one of the most incredible scenes of his life —the mysterious tango.

Jared signed up for three beginning tango series in the same week. He chose one class because of its proximity and the other two because of the appearance of the female teachers. In one of the classes he was surprised to find that there were two extra single guys. This resulted in the unexpected benefit of frequent dances with the teacher, a tall and well-endowed mix of African and Puerto Rican blood that he had been mesmerized by at the dance that introduced him to tango. In heels, Stella, the teacher, was an inch taller than Jared. They shared four points of contact, left hand to her right hand, opposite arms wrapped against each other, and the two points of her insurmountable chest that he was instructed to keep in front of.

Following the first series of classes he took a private lesson with all three female teachers and then signed up for four more series that he would take simultaneously. Jared knew he couldn't depend on his looks to temper the cut of an unpleasant dance experience. He would earn his place with the women of his dreams by talent. Though tempted, he didn't attend any dances during either the first or second groups of classes.

Sabrina sat across Jared's lap, still wearing a gold shimmering dress that advertised boldly of the pleasures within; money was all it took to let Jared into the pleasures of Sabrina's skin. Dancing tango with a woman required such concentration, months of learning and practice. Sabrina, or any other girl of a sex club, gave an instantaneous rush of pleasure, a sensual honey on-demand right from the tap, shut-off again as soon as the money stopped coming. "I've missed you. You found some girl across town that you like better than me?"

"No. I haven't been to a club since I saw you last." Sabrina licked her lips shiny and put one arm around his neck. For the first time in over a year, Jared had saved a thousand dollars at the end of a month.

"Somebody giving you what you want at no charge?"

"I've been learning to tango."

Dropping the straps off of her shoulders she said, "Sounds hot. Tell me about it."

"I'm not very good yet, but I'm taking all the classes I can get."

Sabrina edged the thin golden veneer down to her waist. "So what's the big deal about this tango?"

"I stumbled upon this dance, actually, it was the same night that I last saw you. People looked so…excited. Or, alive."

"And lots of beautiful women?"

"Yeah."

"Do they make you feel excited like this?" At the pronouncement of this delicate question, Sabrina momentarily broke the club rules and slipped her hand down between Jared's legs to perhaps exhibit an advantage of being with her versus his tango partners. Next, she removed her dress.

Jared attended his first milonga the weekend after finishing his second round of classes and another complement of private lessons. He was pleased with himself; he believed he was getting the tango and could execute everything he had been shown. So why, as he stood by the floor and watched the flow of dancers before him, was he so scared?

Sweating and feeling like an unseen kid at an adult party, Jared scanned the floor and sidelines for a potential partner. He recognized only two couples from all of his classes and no singles, at least no women. These two couples tangoed just with their partners, sitting hand-in-hand until they danced again. He let his eyes rest on one of them, a woman in her early twenties. He felt such a rush of desire for her that it wasn't until the third time they danced in class that he could relax enough to dance to his best ability. She leaned into her tall friend, a young man with wavy black hair and broad chest, and curled her arm into his as they sat in a booth. Jared couldn't imagine why she might want to dance with him instead of the man at her side.

Jared watched feet for awhile. Most people weren't doing anything complicated. All he had to do was dance what he knew and he'd be like all the rest. Single women were numerous. At the beginning of every dance they dotted the landscape like stands of flowers. Jared ordered his second drink and drank it fast, tequila and sweet lime juice.

He had to choose. The men ask the women. Maybe this was best. Jared realized he would hate to be stuck with only those that would choose him, a short scrawny white guy with deep recessed eyes and tiny mouth. What if the woman he asked said no? Should he choose from the small pool of lesser attractive women? A woman in her sixties sat by herself. He hadn't seen her dance yet. She would probably be grateful. Or would she be embarrassed to dance with someone almost thirty years younger? He wasn't here to dance with his mother, he told himself. A small woman stood not far from him. She was close to his age, probably mid-forties, wearing black pants and a tan silk blouse that did nothing for her. Maybe she would be a good start. He set his drink down and started walking over towards her. Another woman came up along side of her, sipping from a glass. The new woman was only about thirty, with long bare legs and a back-less dress. The shorter woman saw Jared approach. He gave her a quick smile and broke eye contact. "Would you like to dance?"

Jared's hand on her elbow, the taller woman looked towards him, her eyes lowering from the top of his head to his eyes. "All right."

She stepped in close, easily wrapping her left arm all the way around his shoulders. Jared placed his right hand on her warm bare back and her chest jumped into him with a quick exhale. "Your hand's cold," she said.

"Sorry, I was holding a cold drink." He backed his hand off, only making contact with his arm.

"It's okay. It was just a reflex."

She settled back into him. Her breasts nudging upwards, seemingly just under his chin. He could only see straight ahead and to his left. He had danced with tall women before, but only in classes with lots of room on the floor. Fortunately, the most basic opening step is to the left and he took it. One more step forward and his path was blocked. He wasn't balanced and had to slide his feet.

"Go ahead and hold your hand against me like you normally would. It wasn't painful before, the cold just startled me."

His palm cupped her shoulder blade, which massaged against his hand, now flat, now jutting out and spreading to his fingers. Her curly brown hair draped the right side of his face, sweet blossom scented strands dancing across his nose and mouth. She was standing so close! Everywhere he touched was hot luxurious skin. All he said was, "do you want to dance." She wanted to be here. Or, at least, she wanted to be here with somebody, somebody that could dance. There's always a price to pay, he thought to himself. He could dance. Couldn't he? They danced close in class, but not like this. He stepped forward in a simple walking step. People were all around him, doing a lot more than he had realized on the sidelines. It was like gazing on the ocean from afar and not having a clue how tall those little white lines of foam are until you're out there in a dinghy. And he couldn't see to his right at all. It was his job to keep track of what foot she was on, but she stepped so lightly it was hard to tell. With the slightest of side maneuvering she was crossing her feet and twisting her hips around him. Someone bumped him from behind. They ran into a couple on his right side while walking straight! What was this woman thinking who still held on to him like a lover? Did a woman ever just leave a partner and walk off the floor in the middle of a dance?

Yet Jared didn't want the song to end. He wanted half the people to leave the floor. Or better yet, hear his partner suggest that they drift off to somewhere quiet and explore how many places they can hold tight to the other. On the way to the bathrooms was a small practice floor where he saw two couples dancing. Would she join him there? They bumped someone again. He'd better concentrate. God, she must be bored. He knew more steps than he was leading her through, but he needed a running start at them, room to plan. The song ended. Everyone catching the last beat except for him. He feared the look on her face.

"Sorry we bumped into some people," Jared offered.

"I know, I'm hard to see around with my hair."

"No. I mean…this was one of my first dances…actually my very first besides classes." So he'd done it, shown his hand. He was just a beginner. As if he was fooling anybody. Up close, he could see that she was older than he had thought. Maybe even a little older than he was.

"I'm glad I don't have to lead," was the remainder of her comments. A new song began. She slipped back into his arm. Jared stood dumbfounded. She hadn't walked away when she had the chance. He knew of the convention of dancing three or four songs with each partner; it wasn't necessary though. They danced again. It wasn't easier than the first time, but maybe he had done all right.

"Thank you. My name's Angela."

Jared fumbled for an expression to accompany what he was feeling. "Dancing is harder on a crowded floor."

"You danced great for the first time. Keep at it and you'll do just fine. See you at other milongas." She started to turn.

"Would you like a drink?" he asked.

"No thank you." Angela spun on one foot and the sea of dancers parted before her. Couples swirled around him like a rising tide as Jared darted through narrow openings. Safely back on shore, he could turn to the call of his dry throat. Not being able to recognize his glass of ice in the dim, he ordered another.

With the cold liquid trickling down inside, he could take a look at what had just passed. Why had this enticing woman been so kind?

She couldn't possibly have enjoyed being stumbled around the floor when she's use to gliding, especially with a frump like him. So what was in it for her? Jared concluded that she must be the type that's unavoidably considerate.

Jared watched the next series of dances standing by the side of the floor. He decided that he wasn't proficient enough for this level of dancing and would return after another month of classes. Taking the last chip of ice and crunching it to liquid, he turned to return his glass to the bar. Standing only five feet off was the woman in the tan blouse. Had she been there for the last half-hour? He hadn't noticed her dancing, but some people stand out more than others. She caught him staring and gave a smile with lowered eyes. Geez, he thought, this is the second time she's seen me looking her over and not asking her to dance. With the warmed glass still in his hand, he went to her.

"I would ask you to dance, but this is my first milonga and I embarrassed myself about a half-hour ago."

"We've all been beginners before. I would be happy to get out on the floor again."

"I can't imagine that it would be any fun for you to dance with me."

"I'll take that chance."

"All right, but don't say I didn't warn you."

Her face came into focus. Soft rounded cheeks supported small wide spaced eyes. Thin lips opened only enough to let the words escape. She was even shorter than he thought from a few feet away, her head not quite fitting under his chin. She brought her chest a breath away from his and waited. Three steps into the throng and Jared wished he had just left. He stepped on her foot.

"Sorry."

"It doesn't hurt." But she had flinched.

Walking, his teachers all said that it was the hardest part of tango. Now he understood. So often, there wasn't anywhere to go because of dancers on every side. He side-stepped and rock-stepped until he was even boring himself. Somewhere, his head held the code for a few more steps, but he was blank, couldn't think of anything. At last, the final note of the current song.

"Told you. I'm not just a beginner, I'm brain dead. Even the stuff I know I can't remember."

"It's extra tough when it's so crowded." She didn't let his hand go. "Hear the music? It's a modern tango." A lone bandoneon crept up a wayward scale and was setting the stage for two people to forget about all else besides the person in their arms. "It's a very slow song without much rhythm. You could dance it with only ten steps."

"I don't even know that many."

"I don't mean ten step patterns, just moving your feet ten times. Ten actual steps."

"I don't understand."

"Here." She led him a few feet to the center of the floor. "In the center, we don't need to travel at all. I know classes teach a lot of patterns, but tango isn't about how many times you go around the floor." Her eyes suddenly dropped. Jared wondered if she was afraid that she had gone too far. If *she* was in over her head, then they would drown as a couple for sure. She took one little step and her chest was tight against him. Raising her mouth close to his ear she said, "Feel the music and only step when it says you have to."

Dance to the music, all teachers had said this. Step on the beat and use the emotionality of the individual song in your interpretation. She knew nothing about him except that he was a beginning dancer. What was she expecting? Why would she put such trust in him?

A violin told him to hold tighter. Jared bent his knees slightly and shifted his chest and arms to support her. Letting his eyes drift, he saw that no one was watching them. Most of the women had their eyes closed. The men had slowed the pace of the dance. Surrounded by entwined couples, no one on the sidelines could see them at all. He raised his arm into her back and she elongated against him. He set her on her left foot and there she stayed, seemingly uninterested in doing anything else. Twisting her, he noticed that all she did was pivot on her one foot. A plucked cello string suggested only inner movement, not traveling. The bandoneon released each note with reluctance like wax on the edge of a thick candle, dripping, but not disappearing. Squeezing her chest to his, he took a step around her, then another. All the while she stayed on one foot pivoting while he circled her.

A piano struck chords at the same time a few feet opened up behind his partner and he led her into the void onto her other foot. Hair brushed his lips with the scent of honeysuckle. The fingers of her warm hand clutched his neck. Her chest rose and fell against his as if she were lying on top of him. He would twist her gently and her free foot played with his ankle. He thought of Sabrina and Michaela and how their bodies felt and the only thing that struck him as being different was that this woman wanted to be here with him right now. The same broiling sea of cresting dancers and reefs of sharp heels was for a minute, a calm harbor.

Releasing into the quiet, Jared barely recognized the woman that emerged from his hold. He might not have given her a second look on the street. Now it hurt to let her go. "You didn't even take all ten steps," she said and he thought he noticed her blush. A fast song started with a brash bouncy beat. "You don't know the Milonga style yet do you?" she said, referring to the music. Jared shook his head. "I wouldn't think so this early. Let's get off the floor before we become a hazard."

"I had a feeling that we'd do all right together," she said. "I enjoyed that. Thank you."

"I didn't know you could do that," Jared replied and they both broke into laughter, released into the gay buoyancy of the current music.

"Most people will tell you that fewer steps are a better bet most of the time, whatever your name is."

"Sorry, I'm Jared."

"Tricia." They shook hands, so oddly casual after what they had just shared. It accented the fact that he knew so little about her, though for a blessed moment, he had everything he wanted.

"Would you like a drink, Tricia?"

"No thanks. But I hope to dance with you often in the months to come. See ya." With a squeeze of his hand, she was off. She didn't go far, just twenty feet away to wait for the next request to dance.

Jared watched as couples relished the light exuberance of the

Milonga style, so different from most of the tango music played in any regular evening. He breathed deep and freely. Someone asked Tricia to dance and he was happy for her. He wanted to learn how to dance to all the music and meet all these beautiful people. Walking out into the night, he forgot his coat.

Jared's apartment greeted him with an invisible wave of stale pizza. He gathered up the cheese-encrusted box and overflowing trashcan and took them to the bin outside. Returning briefly to the cold was when he remembered his coat. Hunger took him to the pantry, where he scored a box of cereal. Out of milk, he mixed up some frozen orange juice to moisten the flakes.

Tangy spoonful at a time, he thought of his two dance partners and felt embarrassed. He had been taken care of by these two women. Angela probably wouldn't even remember him in a month. Tricia wouldn't forget, but like a mother, she had held his wobbly hand and kept him on the slide when he was afraid of the height. What would it take to be the strong one? To be the leader? If proceeding through fear requires courage, he could at least give himself that.

The clay torso lay with a cloth on it, untouched for several months. He ran his fingers down the naked breasts and onto the belly. Neither woman had accepted his offer for a drink. Maybe that was normal. Maybe when he was a good dancer there'd be more interest. He traced down past the hips to the thighs, which ended in muddle. It didn't seem right anymore that she didn't have feet and he started warming clay from the fridge.

"Jared? It's Mom." Jared had worked until four in the morning shaping feet on the sculpture. When the phone rang, he was tangoing on a crowded floor in the Argentina of his mind. His partner was holding him tighter and tighter. He looked down to check for her feet and saw that he didn't have pants on, only a pair of briefs. Racked in the mystery of where his trousers had fled, or if he had come without them, and how he was going to continue unnoticed, the phone shocked him awake, momentarily masquerading as a fire alarm in his dream. For a moment, *tangueros* were running for the door. On the fourth ring he had managed to lift the receiver and hear his mother's voice. He peered over the pillow at the red digital display. Eight-thirty.

"Good morning."

"You sound asleep?"

"I worked late."

"You've got a job?"

"No. On a sculpture. I came home from tango dancing and felt like working."

"I'm glad somebody is having fun."

"Yeah, I guess. How are you mom?"

She didn't answer right away. "Tired."

It was only eleven-thirty even in Florida. "Did you sleep last night?"

"I woke up at two feeling so cold and couldn't get back to sleep. I need to sell this house and find somewhere with more people around."

"I think that's a good idea."

"Will you help me move?"

Florida is strange to Californians, even for those that have only lived on the west coast a short while. Without mountains to orient oneself, you have to learn your way around by rote, memorizing street names or at least the buildings on them. Tall geography helps to remind you of the big picture. In Florida, the only grand vistas while standing on soil are over the ocean, which is usually so calm that it doesn't look near as ominous as it is. Then a hurricane threatens everything and the whole state endures the inevitable onslaught of nature. In California, the temperature often varies fifty degrees in fifty miles and fierce storms might never breach a mountain ridge. How each person reacts to these differences is hard to predict, but most people seek a topography that suits them. Jared's mother, Diana, was living with a personal hurricane bearing down on her fragile shoreline.

Jared steered his rental car past the gated entry to "Shoreline Vistas" and marveled at the uniformity of wealth. Enormous bright gray condominiums undulated over the flatland like rows of teeth.

Diana's door was locked, so Jared had to wait until she made her way to open it. The door appeared to be wood, but the wrap of his knuckles revealed the sound of a plastic skin over a foam core. A foot-high piece of decorative glass with a brass flower adorned the middle. The latch clicked and a small face rimmed with black hair replaced the fancy glass. Diana was wrapped in a thick white cardigan, notwithstanding the fact that Jared found the morning warm enough for shirt sleeves and the air coming from his mother's house was warmer than the outside. Her face-lift had pulled a few years out of her cheeks while the disease in her lungs competed for the air she needed to live. He stepped inside, not needing an invitation, and she leaned a cheek towards him for a kiss while he held her for an instant by the shoulders.

"Was your flight all right?" she asked.

"I slept most of it." His mom didn't look the same, but he couldn't say what the difference was. She had dyed her hair ever since it had started to gray, so that wasn't it. Maybe she was shorter, though he doubted it. Something about her face—not the face-lift, either, made her look like someone other than his mother.

"You're still tired. You can go sleep for a few hours in the guest room."

"No Mom, I'm great, really. So you're ready to leave this cookie-cutter mansion for a raging single's commune?"

"It's too much for me. I feel like a marble in a refrigerator box." Diana smiled, coughed, and brought one hand up to her face. She closed her eyes tight and concentrated on quieting her chest. "I stopped smoking two days ago." She patted her arm. "I've got the patch."

"That's good mom. That's really good."

After lunch in the condominium, Jared took her to look at homes with a social context, group living situations. Some of them catered to the elderly, people at least ten years older than his mom, although several of the septuagenarians bounded by with far more energy than Diana. A couple of the community complexes sported younger residents, recently retired transplants, many of whom still maintained another home in a northern state.

For dinner, Diana took her son out to the "Laissez-Faire" seafood restaurant by the water. Diana had only picked at her lunch, but had no trouble slipping down her half of the oysters and they ordered another dozen. Jared squeezed lemon over the second group and dabbled horseradish onto one, lifted, and let it slide onto his tongue.

"So what is it about this tango dance that has you spell-bound?" his mom asked.

Caught in the full mouth moment of sour, bitter, and sweet flesh, he took the time to think his response. To just say that it was fun wouldn't be any more complete or revealing than to say that the reason he liked oysters was that they were wet. "It's as good as any way I've ever known to be with a woman."

"You're getting out and meeting women again—that's good."

"There are many ways to *meet* women. Meeting them is easy. Tango is such a wonderful way to *be* with a woman."

"Oh?" He didn't know where his mom's mind was racing; maybe she thought that this was a private topic. She coughed into her napkin until the fit passed. Jared sensed they were standing at a doorway they'd never crossed. Thirty years ago, she had been the largest element in his life. For the last fifteen, she had been a footnote. He realized in a flash that what was different about her face was that he first saw the face of a woman, only later taking her in as his mother. And a woman that he only knew in one limited way. Diana continued before Jared could get the words together, "I guess it's important for men and women to have something that they enjoy doing together..." she hesitated, looking awkward at what could be read into her statement, and elaborated, "...when they're first getting to know each other."

"Yes, but tango isn't just an alternative to going on Sierra Club hikes. It cuts through all of the relationship stuff and creates a space for each of us to...love and care for the other."

"Dancing has always been a mating ritual, especially the slow stuff."

"But that's just it—tango isn't about what comes *after* the dance. It's only about the time you're on the floor together."

"Then you're not seeing any of these tango women?"

"No. Although I have tried. That's when I learned that tango wasn't a mating game."

They both reached for a last oyster. The tray of empty shells and stained ice was whisked away. Soon, they were staring at their chosen crustacean, Jared with Cajun-spiced prawns and Diana with the flagship of sea-bottom cuisine, lobster.

The next day, Jared took his mother to a doctor's appointment. Diana was tired from all of the previous day's activities and looked sicker. The doctor applauded Diana for having quit smoking and told Jared on the side that her chances were reasonably good if she never smoked again, but terrible if she lit-up.

Diana fell asleep after lunch and Jared toured senior living facilities on his own. One looked promising with its claims of fun-filled activities—pot lucks, games, parties, and assistance with house maintenance and transportation. His mom, at sixty-three, would be one of the younger residents. Jared had trouble imagining Diana amongst this group, especially since his father was still so vital and the father of three young kids. Maybe he would take his mother to look at this one when he returned in a week from the Denver tango festival.

Jared brought home take-out Thai for dinner. Diana was sitting at the kitchen table in front of a Metropolitan Home. She was wearing a house coat over something bulky and no make-up. "Seems a shame to settle for an apartment when one could create beautiful living spaces." Jared searched for words, but his mother continued. "Why am I alone, Jared?" He looked at her face which reminded him of a parched house plant. "Did I do something wrong?"

"No Mom. Nobody did anything wrong."

Diana stood up, started to refill her soda at the counter and said, "Being right is probably way overrated anyway." She put the bottle down and stared blankly at the counter. Her lips tightened and the first tear escaped.

The chair screeched on the floor as Jared slid it back. He touched her shoulder. "Mom."

"I'm so scared. How do I be strong?"

She stood hunched over the counter, still not looking at him. Jared rubbed her back, or at least the many layers that covered it. Her head tilted towards him. He pried her hand off of the soda bottle and turned her into him, rested her head on his shoulder and encircled her with both arms. For a moment, her arms hung limp at her sides. Then she raised her tiny hands and wrapped them as far as they went around his back. Jared couldn't remember the last time that they had hugged for more than a second, and that was always in greeting. Maybe when he was ten years old? He held her until the hummingbird within all the clothing began to stir. They separated a few inches.

"It takes strength just to go on. Being happy while you do it is the hardest part," Jared said. "Maybe you should get an apartment near me in San Francisco."

"Even the summers there are too cold for me."

"Okay then, we'll find you a place in this funny state with a lot of eccentric seniors around to keep you entertained."

"I'll be all right. Maybe I just needed a hug."

Jared shifted his weight in the aisle seat as the jet reached cruising altitude over the Deep South. He glanced back one row and across the aisle at a couple he had sat near while waiting to board. Really, he was just keeping track of the woman. She had a delectably pretty face under short bright red hair. An unbuttoned shirt with a diminutive flesh-tone bra underneath, gave the frequent illusion of nothing but bare skin.

"Would you like something to drink, Sir?" the flight attendant asked him. She was about his age, immaculately manicured, with shoulder-length blonde hair set off by the navy blue airline uniform. Her face make-up created an entirely homogenous skin-tone, highlighted by only a hint of cheek blush. What would she be like to tango with? If she had a taste of the dance, would it awaken a sleeping hunger and send her into a feast of classes? Would she hold onto him like a lover, chest to chest for fifteen minutes of a tango set? Or would she still usually prefer to be alone in a quiet hotel room with a mystery novel?

Jared knew he was being selfish leaving his mother for the week while attending the tango festival; he had never seen her with such little strength. But he had finally found something that he loved enough so that the rest of his life made sense. Was his mother dying? Did she get sick to see if anybody cared? Jared didn't hold much belief in such a "New Age" concept, but he couldn't dismiss it entirely. It would at least require a good deal of care to keep her around. Jared thought of the long hug he had given Diana yesterday and wondered if it had been appropriate for a mother and son. Had she ever failed to show love in return? Well, yes, at least in the way he would have preferred it.

Wasn't his mother also struggling to find something that made her happy? What if she, like him, found tango and added it to her life? Wouldn't this give her everything she lacked? Community? Partners that cherished her life for a few dependable minutes every week? Perhaps, but this wouldn't cure her lungs. Maybe something as life-encompassing as tango was too much for her right now. What if she would have found tango five years ago? In a couple of years she might be well enough to try it. Would sixty-five be too old to begin tango? He promised himself to check out tango classes in her area when he returned.

It struck Jared as odd that he was probably the only person on this jet of three hundred that knew how to tango. What if his country tangoed like they watched sports or the nightly television serial? He was sure that there were entire states where the tango would not be danced this whole month.

And Sabrina, lap-dancing her way through college—how was she? Jared hadn't seen her in over a month.

He glanced back at the couple across the aisle and behind him. The woman and man lay with their heads nestled against each other, the open gap in her blouse revealing all that was legal. Seeing her aroused a number of desires in Jared, but the trusting lean of her head on her partner's shoulder was the one he wanted most.

Tango and Those Other Dances

Why isn't everybody drawn to the tango? At the very least, why doesn't everybody who partner dances (lead and follow, step to the same rhythm…) want to dance the tango? I understand those who want to tango but never try because they are afraid they won't be able to learn it within the time frame they're willing to give it. I see the fear in their eyes as they back peddle from putting their egos to the test, only to fail. I'm talking about highly capable men and women, too, people who can command large audiences to listen to them speak and others who can climb mountains or build mansions. The ones who surprise me are those who get a good look at Argentine tango and truly don't want it in their lives, even if all they had to do was take a pill.

Those who know how to tango within our large country of the United States of America are a lone bandoneon in a coliseum of electric guitars. Yet, even just counting those who partner dance, *tangueros* are still only one car on a long train. Why is that? Once I got Argentine tango's essence, I stopped taking classes in all the other dances. I admit that it took me three attempts at introductory tango classes before I felt what the tango had to offer, but once the taste came through I was determined to learn its recipe, however long it took. Sure, when the salsa band is in town I still go out and have a great time without tango, but that's only because I live in a small town and there isn't a tango venue that night. If I were nearer to San Francisco, I would only need a small room for sleeping because I wouldn't get much use out of my apartment—mild mannered day laborer and tango night hawk.

Why are there hundreds of thousands who can salsa and swing and two step and relatively few *tangueros?* What draws people to one type of dance instead of another? One glaring reason is that tango is difficult; it takes many months of dancing twice a week (preferably one night with a class) to scale the height of the first step in a long winding staircase. To grasp the illusive subtleties will challenge the strongest of egos. Like the unflinching beat of a Di Sarli tango, the beginning *tanguero* (a very long lasting title) is reminded ad nauseam to "lead with the chest, keep your partner in front of you, stretch your leg out straight behind you from the hip, always bring your feet together before the next step," and on and on. Add to this the fact that tango is not about interspersing more complicated step patterns between basic steps, which is how most all the other dances are approached. Occasionally American teachers will try to simplify tango to this mostly memorized parts-and-pieces mode which American ballroom students are familiar with, but this guts the tango of its soul — the art of improvisation within the strict confines of body connection. So much to infuse into the recesses of our muscles so that we can give our attention over to the music and the partner wrapped in our arms. It takes at least five years of constant dedication in an environment abundant with teachers before one comes to the place where he no longer feels he still has a vast amount to learn.

Foxtrot

Having said this, I must also admit tango isn't any more challenging than the foxtrot if one is determined to dance the foxtrot at competition standards. It's just easier to fake the foxtrot, take a four week class, grab your partner, and get out on the floor and do *something*.

Maybe it's the music that is the primary calling to a dance. Foxtrot music, Frank Sinatra and the Big Bands of the 1940s, is still much more accessible to the average American. The tempo is a steady saunter down the sidewalk, the mood is upbeat even when the girl is leaving him, and, after all, the words are in English. Tango music is dangerous, even if the clubs are now safe. You don't have to know Spanish to realize that in every other song something isn't okay, in fact, there is misery, the singer won't recover easily, and it's not a story for kids. The bandoneon won't let you be content in a life void of passion; it will pry open your heart and drag it from one side of the floor to the other until you take in other hearts around you. A lot of Americans just want to dress up, go out, and have a little light fun; for them, the foxtrot might be the best match.

Still, there is also a level of foxtrot that conjures images of Fred Astaire and Ginger Rogers, tuxedos, gowns, and high society. Full blown competition level foxtrot demands a large ballroom to perform its grandiose sweeping turns for a demanding, critical audience. To be an accomplished foxtrotter at that level requires the same determination as the tango. Acquaintances have told me of the thousands of dollars of private lessons it took to master the feather, twinkle, and heel turns of the foxtrot. In truth, the number of *tangueros* has probably already surpassed the number of serious foxtrotters in the United States.

American and International Tango (Ballroom Tango)

Anyone who has seen competitive ballroom dancing on PBS television has witnessed the excesses of "International ballroom style tango," that is, the crisply military change of direction, the stiffly outstretched hands leading a charge, accompanied by vertebrae-crunching head snapping. Even though hip bones may be grinding against one another and thighs are making contact with groins, the dancers' well-coiffed heads are held far apart. They are dancing for audience and judges, not for each other. This style of tango is the one we described as having been created in Europe and codified primarily by the British.

American style tango, while having evolved from International tango rather than from Argentine tango, is a bit more relaxed, versatile, and romantic than its European counterpart, as are most American style ballroom dances. But it too bears little resemblance to the Argentine original. We know of no one who has delved deeply into Argentine tango and still chooses to dance ballroom style, even on an occasional basis.

Who would prefer ballroom tango to Argentine? Ballroom tango is very difficult; one wouldn't choose it for simplicity sake. Maybe it's the crowd you hang-out with. You can add ballroom tango to foxtrot, waltz, and the rest of the mixed ballroom scene and not have to change dance halls. Maybe it's what you're comfortable with, especially in public. I am reminded of a comparison I read in a <u>Smithsonian</u> article on tango about twelve years ago. A man was quoted as saying something like this: American tango is like a new relationship; both the man and woman are on their best behavior, never mind the dishonesty. Let's just not upset anyone. Argentine tango is like a mature relationship, full of passion, but with each person expressing his or her needs and carving out their identity. International tango is where the couple is only still together for the sake of the kids.

Swing

Swing, born in the United States in the 1920s, is the epitome of positive outgoing American spirit. Merging the music and cultures of African and European Americans like nothing had before, it took over the popular scene during the 1930s and lasted well into the 50s. Then, in the late 90s, it was all the rage again.

Swing dancing is about having fun. There are thousands of skilled dancers who take the swing very seriously, but if you're serious when you dance swing, you've missed the heart of the dance. Oh, I know all about West Coast swing and the slow get down blues music with tales of heartbreak, but just because they aren't smiling as much as the Lindy hoppers doesn't mean that it still isn't about the fun. And if you find yourself in a Frankie Manning workshop and see five hundred people getting infused with the man's indefatigable love of life expressed in the Lindy Hop swing, your mood lifts like it never had weight to start with. I have had many fun moments dancing tango, but fun is an incidental reward of the whole tango experience.

There is one large similarity between swing and tango that causes a lot of crossover in both directions; tango and swing (Lindy Hop, jitterbug, West Coast, doesn't matter…) dances were created with a flexible form that demands *improvisation*. Listen to the music and let it tell you what to do next. Ballroom dancers will correctly tell you that they also dance to interpret the music, but they don't stop in the middle of a waltz and "horse around." Swing dancers cruise along at a 140 beats a minute until that break in the music when the chord progression recapitulates or all the instruments drop out for a few bars while the drums rock or the saxophone boils over and the dancers play, shake their hips, point their fingers at each other, engaging in whatever theatrical nonsense that they feel like in the moment. Tango, too, is laced with these moments many times in every song. In tango though, comedy is a rare expression. When the rhythm pauses and you careen down an emotional slope to the run of a violin, tango dancers caress with arms, hands, feet, chests, cheeks, we show we are glad that the other person is alive.

The Latin Dances

The dances best equipped to match the tango in its pure heat of intimate excitement are the Afro-Cuban family of salsa and rumba and the Brazilian samba and bolero. The rumba and bolero are slow and sultry, creating an atmosphere of smoking embers which erupt briefly into flame and die back down to shimmering heat. The faster salsa, samba, and merengue are a burning blaze from start to finish. The tango is frequently all of this in the same song, combined with the pauses described above in the section on swing. Tango, though, adds a level of intimacy not found in any other dance in the close embrace.

Most of the Latin dances (rumba, salsa, merengue and bolero) are relatively easy to grasp the basics of and get onto the floor with. The ballroom style samba is the exception. It is exceedingly difficult to perform at normal speed and few there are that do it well with an extensive vocabulary. It is fast and aerobic, which explains part of the challenge. The other tricky nuance of samba is the syncopated beat which requires extra concentration. It is the music of Carnival and liberal frivolity.

A Postscript Observation

We end this survey of "those other dances" with one last observation. Why isn't Argentine tango labeled a Latin dance, even though it originated in Latin America? One reason is that until recently, tango's partially African roots were not given attention, or even credence, and so tango appears not to fit the Afro-Latin profile of other Latin dances which proudly proclaim their African roots. But the major reason, we would venture, is that tango, *unlike* all the other Latin dances, forbids hip action. The more pronounced African roots that mark the other Latin dances with loose, swingy hip movement in all directions is noticeably absent in tango. Instead, tango posture is erect and restrained, the lead proceeding from the upper torso, the hips held still and quiet above legs that, in contrast, may be wildly active. It is this absence of hip action, perhaps, or so claim some tango historians, that made tango seem more European than African to refined early 20th century Europeans, and therefore less racially threatening than those hip swinging dances originating in Africa. The question of why hip action would seem more threatening than tango's close embrace and intertwined thighs—a level of intimacy not before seen in partnered social dancing—may be another of those mystery ingredients in tango's historical recipe.

Chapter 2

The Reality

What you see when you watch a tango

IF YOU'RE NEW to a milonga, the tangos you see whizzing by you at first don't look so different from ballroom dances you may know as the waltz and foxtrot and American tango. The dancers embrace and move more or less in dance direction (line of dance or counter clockwise) around the floor. But stand still and watch more closely, and you'll see how different tango is.

The European embraced dances, danced by Argentine immigrants in the early twentieth century, evolved into something that no one could have predicted once they were brought to the New World. Of course, knowing something about the exotic cultures these Europeans collided with in this new setting, and the sexual tension related to the paucity of women, helps to explain at least some features of the dance.

Closer observation reveals, for example, that the man's steps and the woman's step are clearly different; it may not even be immediately clear that the man is leading the woman's step. But he is. He impels the coordination of the two with his lead, in Spanish called the *marca,* which usually leads her to a *figura,* a response in the form of her step which may look different from what he is doing. *Marca,* though, translated as "lead" doesn't quite correspond to the "lead" of ballroom dances.

The *marca* is three things; the first two are familiar: the slight pressure of the leader's hand against the followers back, and the signals his left hand gives her right hand, which is resting with some slight resistance against his. Ballroom dance technique refers to the maintaining of these two features with firmness and energy as maintaining the dancers' "frame." These qualities of the lead in tango are not so different from European dances where maintaining "frame" is also required for lead and follow. What is different about tango, although also controlled by the lead, is the relationship of the dancers' bodies to each other.

You will notice that leader's and follower's legs seem to move independently of their bodies and also independently of each other's legs. You might see one of the follower's legs suddenly shoot out and whip into a circle before returning to step with the leader's. How did she know to do that, you wonder, when his legs are doing something else? Their torsos are held upright and motionless, all the action seems to be in the legs. But the leader doesn't seem to be leading with his leg steps, as some European dances call for because, you notice, the leader can stop, and hold a position while the follower moves in front of him, or the leader can pivot in place while the follower moves around him.

And this independence of movement is truly what signals one of the unique features of Argentine tango lead. It is a convention of the dance that the follower keeps her chest parallel to the leader's. It is therefore his chest that is the primary "mover" in the lead. As his chest moves, so moves her body into place, always attempting to keep hers parallel. And it is holding their frames firmly and consistently—their hands and arms never leaving their position—that allows them to move together harmoniously, even if differently. Having said that, based on the instruction we have received for close-embrace *milonguero* style, we've observed lately that many of the most experienced dancers use a slight V shaped embrace for all close-embrace dancing; that is, the man's right chest is lined up with woman's breast bone. Try them both, is the best advice. The main objective is to be lined up in an embrace that allows for dancing together in such a well-connected manner that you move as one person. Since the lead is from chest and not the feet, the leader can move his partner without moving himself (his feet, that is); his concentration can be totally on her, on directing her with him or around him. Some men liken it to the pleasure of "driving her" as if she were a luxurious car. Some Argentine teachers even use the verb "to drive," *manejar,* to refer to leading. And some women admit to enjoying the pleasure of being elegantly "driven," of being precisely perfect in their response to the driver. There is potentially immense satisfaction for both dancers.

But if one expects the lead in tango to resemble even vaguely the lead in other social dances, one's expectations are finally dashed at observing the dancer's interpretation of the music. Remember the earlier reference to the tango dancer's option of dancing his feelings, his personal responses to the music. Well, that option includes NOT dancing to the music, something never permitted to the leader of other dancers—unless by default to a toleration of incompetence. But in tango, the tolerance for improvisation on the leader's part overrides all other considerations of the music. If the leader chooses to dance a figure that matches his response to the music and it is a figure that doesn't match the musical beat in a conventional way, well, he has that prerogative. Another of his prerogatives is to stop abruptly, pause, hold a pose, perhaps play with his partner's foot, give her time and space to perform an adornment of her own, or subtly shift her weight in preparation for the next figure.

Tango as a Language

Tango has been described as a language, a body language where every move of the body gives a message that results in some response. It's not uncommon for people to describe tango figures as a conversation between two people. As in most conversations the participants aren't sure of what the next topic will be or how intense the feelings will be about each topic covered. In tango the "topic" will be determined both by the music and the feelings of each dancer in response to the music. Like a conversation's progress from an opening, some dialogue, and toward an ending, moving toward a resolution of a conversation can be likened to the progress of the dance. The leader's intention is a kind of persuasive argument he presents to his partner, and for which he awaits a response. Both know the music will end, conversation over. Since the convention demands that dancing stop with the last note, the leader must be prepared to end the conversation suddenly yet gracefully, and, he hopes, having successfully persuaded his follower of his point (please dance with me again).

Las Diferencias

While a conversation, in its ideal form, can lead to agreement on a topic, almost any conversation *about* Argentine tango is about contrasts, some set of dramatic differences or disagreements, one polarity or other, between this… and that. The contrast between Argentine tango and European-based ballroom dances is only one, and not the most interesting one either. There is the difference between tango and other Latin dances, the dichotomies in tango leading styles and teaching styles, the differences between salon style and club style, and of course the important issues around dominance and submission.

An all-encompassing contrast though, and one which we think determines interesting results, lies in the difference between Argentine tango teachers and their non-Argentine students. Since tango is today popular around the world, and Argentine teachers are imported to do the teaching, they face plenty of variety in their students, some more compatible with them than others. We've heard a few teachers say they experience the most *sympatico* with German tango students. I was surprised to hear this, why Germans? What do Germans have to share with Argentineans? My own biases and the American-held stereotypical German obviously didn't fit with my starry-eyed new admiration of all things Argentine. But further thinking reminded me of young Germans I've met here and abroad.

What they probably share with Argentines are their deep historical melancholy, social ambivalence, distrust of leadership, and the shared experience of disastrous dictatorships. The question makes me want to study tango in Germany with an Argentine *maestro* and dance with German partners, in order to understand them both more intimately and more authentically.

Argentinos and Americanos

Our first teachers, Ed and Barbara Garvey, an older American couple arguably responsible for San Francisco becoming the American capital of tango were introduced to tango through "Tango Argentino" on stage in San Francisco. Determined to learn it for themselves, they began studying with dancers who were connected with the show and who remained in San Francisco. But this was stage tango, they found out when they went to Argentina finally, just a week or two behind Robert Duvall, also determined to find good and authentic tango. This would be the first of nine trips they would make to Buenos Aires in order to study with the *maestros*. Other American friends traveling there before them had given up, deciding tango was not to be found in Buenos Aires. The Garvey's, nothing if not persistent, found the clubs and the musicians. They met a woman who promised to lead them to the best dancers in Buenos Aires. They didn't know it at the time, but later concluded that indeed these dancers she led them to *were* the best, and they *weren't* stage dancers. What they were doing was something the Garvey's hadn't seen — social tango, as it was danced then and now in the clubs. To cap the tour she led, their hostess proudly showed them a photo of herself dancing with Duvall.

To their horror though, this same woman unexpectedly stopped a milonga in order to announce that the guests from Norte Americana would perform for them. Knowing only a diluted shadow of stage tango, they were forced to display it. But something good was to result from their embarrassment in the form of a search for authentic tango. They found it in the elegant instruction of Orlando Paiva and later Nito and Elba, whom they succeeded in bringing to the Bay Area where they are now loved and appreciated. What began, then, with a handful of Americans dancing in their living-rooms before long grew into weekly Bay Area milongas and later week-long tango festivals, at which a series of invited *maestros* regularly presided.

Having now studied with both *maestros* and Americans teachers trained by *maestros*, we have to admit we relish both experiences, but the *maestros* are infinitely more predictable and more fascinating for the insight they give us into their primary cultural sources, even if we don't always learn quite as much as we'd like from them.

First, you can't help noticing the Argentine attitude. They give us Americans, struggling with a new pattern, withering looks as they decide once again they are left to undo damage done us by other teachers or by our own hopeless misconceptions. Americans, they imply, some openly assert, have the impulse to want to look good, but not to see where the origin of a step is—from head *and* heart. Americans seem to want the step packaged and delivered, with as little fuss as possible. Argentine teachers, meanwhile, are determined to convey an entirely different approach to tango and, we must presume, to life.

Americans typically want to learn something quickly and expect to learn something as complex as tango by breaking a pattern down into its parts, practicing the parts in sequence and then practicing more and more of the pattern until the whole is accomplished. They come to a class ready to begin; "enough with these warm ups," their faces weary with impatience tell all: "let's get started, already."

The Argentine teacher will not be rushed. He or she wants to spend time, hopeless though it may be, instilling the "attitude" behind tango into their students: the excruciatingly specific body postures, the inevitable treatises on the "embrace" in all its subtleties, and lectures about how to interpret the feeling of the music, how to accomplish the *marca* and the correct response to it. Meanwhile, Americans new to this inevitably stand, impatient with arms folded across the chest, shifting weight from foot to foot. "When are we gonna get to the dance?" their body language says. And even after the teacher gets the practice going, you can be sure at least one student will stop the action with a challenge, "But so and so famous *maestro* just told us to do it another way. Which way is right?" The pursed up mouth sighing with irritation over inconsistency seems to us our American prerogative. We want things to be simple <u>and</u> consistent. At least that's what Americans learning to tango tend to convey to their foreign teacher. The Classic Culture Clash is alive and well in a tango class.

There is so much Americans don't know, at first anyway, about Argentines, their culture, and their attitude toward the dance that cultural missteps are inevitable. One learns, for example, after studying with a variety of teachers that there are few rules in tango to be consistent about. As for *el maestro* who makes a claim for the correctness of his advice over that of others', it should be remembered that "correctness" in tango is mostly relative, that not only are their different styles dependent on the barrio or academia teachers originated in, but also from their own idiosyncratic take on that style. Americans, if they want to learn to tango beautifully must accept that beauty lies in the feet of the dancer, not in some finite set of rules for correct tango.

If there is any rule to be extracted about tempo, though, an Argentine might say the only rule is to step on an available beat. You can pause as long as you want as long as when you step out again, it's on the beat. Then, watching American couples dance, an Argentine couple will inevitably ask each other "Why are they all rushing?"

The *maestro* takes a deep breath, and tries again to explain where the step comes from. Where in the body it begins, what the leader's intention is, and how to make it unambiguous for the follower. Some teachers will demonstrate a pattern as a gestalt, a whole sequence, refusing to break it down and teach it in parts. It was conceived as a whole and that's how it should be danced and taught, their teaching style asserts. We have personally witnessed the frustration of a *maestro* teaching beginning Americans, many of them with no natural grace or feeling for the music, no internal muscle control to lead from "intention" or from "within." I can't blame any of them, *maestro* or student, for their frustration; it's a given, at first. All *maestros*, happily, discover that some of us don't give up, we <u>do</u> get it; we aren't totally hopeless. But. We will <u>never</u> be Argentines.

One of the most elegant *maestros* of them all, Juan Carlos Copes, voted Argentina's "dancer of the century" is, for all his exquisite dancing, not well understood by Americans as a teacher, precisely because he uses the "gestalt" rather than the breakdown style in teaching figures or patterns. Even though he manages to get around to everyone in a class to demonstrate personally, there are always groups of Americans standing around and watching him, still looking puzzled, waiting for more breakdown of a step, which may never come. The differences in teaching style can be that dramatic. But Copes' remarks about tango are such gems that if students only understand these, they will have learned much from him. In a tango waltz class he was heard to advise: "Don't try to learn fancy waltz steps and then go out on the floor to execute them badly. Dance only the steps you already know, and do them to waltz time. Nothing looks worse than doing steps you don't know, badly." Excellent advice indeed, we've since discovered.

Copes and the other Argentine men we've studied with such as Gavito, Nito, Diego Falco, Fabian Salas, and others all have the unmistakable feline movements of the Argentine male dancers. As resolutely as all American men try to get that style, there are precious few who have actually accomplished it: the long lean cat-like glide with sudden stop and reverse, with an upper torso twist so deep that lower torso is nothing but legs with their freedom to step out suddenly and boldly. It is beautiful to behold, and all the more attractive because of its unique Argentine flavor. As a woman, I find myself wishing more of our American partners had IT.

Why don't they? They have all the requisite body parts, after all, and the natural intelligence that most dancers have no matter where they originate. Of course for men who came of age after 1965, there may be no experience at all with partner dancing and so they are clueless about lead and follow and holding a "frame." But even those who have had significant experience with swing and ballroom can't perfect the male Argentine style. What's missing? Why can't they get IT?

The great, now late, Gavito likes to joke that it's the Argentine male's swaggering stride, mirrored for them by nature and nurture, which is the basis for the leader's style. He exaggeratedly demonstrates the barrio walk that distinguishes a potential *tanguero*, as if it were a natural stroll, and we all laugh. But American women can't help seeing what many American men might see in it... a swish. As another example, he leans against a wall, pretending to smoke, and crosses one ankle over another—tough guy style—to show the genesis of the *cruzada,* the crossed step. We laugh again, it could almost be true, this comic etymology of a dance style. We can't fail to notice, meanwhile, that Argentine men hug and kiss each other openly and effusively, with no suggestion that their affection is anything but manly.

Gavito moving through his paces, wrapping and unwrapping the youthful and luscious Marcela around him, obviously in charge of her and with her full approval, well there's no gender ambivalence about *that*, one could say. Which brings up the opposite end of the male spectrum—the macho extreme. In our American zeal for cultivating gentle men, men firmly in touch with their feminine side and conscious of women's demand for respect, we may have socially bred out of many of them what is natural to men in other cultures—a display of male sexual dominance as a mating ritual, usually meant to be perceived not as demeaning but rather as flattering to women. Indeed, political correctness in America has made it hard for an American *tanguero* to be authentic.

Watch Argentine male dancers as they hold their hips tantalizingly still, then reach out to step out with power and at the same time languorousness, their faces straining with both gravitas and the ecstasy of concentration. (Gavito calls this movement "relax to go, stretch to arrive" and he is astonishingly accurate in this, we discover when physically mimicking those words.) Consider this though: there is no cognate in the experience of America's men, unless maybe they are moving up to a tee or headed for the goal post with hardly a woman in the picture, certainly not in intimate contact. Considering the lack of analog for American men, it's not so surprising that they have trouble acquiring IT. And one more barrier shouldn't be overlooked; the emotions that generated the very first tangos were specific to the Argentine (and perhaps other immigrant) male's experience of dislocation and exclusion. The intensity we see in the body form and faces of male Argentine dancers reflect feelings few American men have experienced: the results of being in touch with ancestral male pain, nostalgia for a home too far away to return to, the pain of social inadequacy, of lack of control over one's destiny. Our emphasis in America on being positive and chipper can be an obstacle to learning to tango. Much more effective, for both leader and follower, is to allow melancholy—whatever its source—to join them on the dance floor and never apologize for it.

> Some other cultural differences, the Argentine teacher Susana Miller points out, are similarly acted out in milongas of Buenos Aires. In an interview she muses on these: "In the U.S. they approach to where you are sitting to invite you to dance, a thing which in Buenos Aires would never occur for fear of rejection. In the U.S... here's not the horrendous fear *porteños* have of ridicule. We are much more fetishist than the American and than any other culture; ridicule for us is an unbearable vertigo situation that we can't stand. Abroad... it's more relaxed, more about friendship. Buenos Aires is very demanding for that strong feeling of who I am in the milonga." (from *Repor Tango*, 2002)

Men and Women

On the topic of lead and follow, both beginning and advanced dancers will be hit with more advice than on any other aspect of tango, and much of it will be contradictory. The perplexed look on the face of an inexperienced dancer when his leading is corrected by a *maestro* is a common sight at workshops. "Stronger lead? But at the last workshop I was told to lighten up my lead!" he might groan. Followers also know from experience there is as much variation among *maestros* as among students in this respect; they also know it is their job to adapt and follow. One of us likened *Maestro* Nito's lead to an ocean liner, another called him the "Cadillac" of leads. From women favoring a strong lead, these are strong compliments indeed. Other followers prefer a more subtle and refined lead. Whatever our preference, we all laugh at Gavito's examples of different leading styles: "*abysmo,* gladiator, and cradle." *Abysmo,* as Gavito caricatures him, is the ultimate wimp. Spaghetti arms, head down, wobbly knees. "Gladiator" moves like a bull in heat, tight grip, trampling his partner as well as everyone in the vicinity. "Cradle" is the leader who literally folds his partner into a womb-like embrace. His embrace gives confidence; his simple but elegant steps are clear and easy to follow.

Our favorite teachers love to chide overeager men by reporting the results of women polled: the man voted most desirable as a partner is the one who leads basic steps beautifully, clearly, confidently rather than the one who tries to dazzle with showy steps that can be ambiguous or difficult to follow precisely. Since the woman's primary role in tango is to be sensitive to the lead, to be always poised on her own axis and ready to physically "read" her partner's message, she wants that message to be crystal clear.

Ready explanations for the uniqueness of Argentine tango lead and follow come from all quarters, including from Argentine social history. Juliet Taylor in her analysis of Argentine tango explains the source of Argentine lead and follow as the "pain" immigrant men felt about their "exclusion" from European society:

> "This embrace can be danced to enact and exaggerate exclusion not inclusion, objectification not intimacy, difference not sameness. In doing so it mirrors exclusions Argentines are vulnerable to at the hands of Europeans. And because they have taken this exclusion in the teeth, they enact exclusion better than its original perpetrators."

She goes a step further to explain, with irony, the later European fascination with the imported tango:

> "A dance of domination like other European embraced dances became an imitation that surpassed the original. The European inventors watched the reproduced rejection and ended imitating the Argentine imitation. Europeans imported teachers. They imported hair pomade. But they never got the violence quite right." (Taylor, *Paper Tangos:* 65-66)

But other writers and explicators make it very clear that the "violence" that Taylor calls a uniquely Argentinean feature in origin, was purposely expurgated from the dance once it hit Paris and London polite societies, and even in expurgated form it was labeled exotic enough to titillate and scandalize and so become all the rage. Perhaps the proximity of chests and the male thigh tight between the woman's legs, were enough to titillate even uninhibited Parisians.

Dominance and Submission

Domination and Submission are powerful coordinates in the map of tango and always a ripple in the undercurrent of conversation among *tangueras,* if not among everyone who does partner dances. There are times in every *tanguera's* dance life when she feels irritation by her more passive role. Being the follower, for example, requires her to follow every leader, even inferior dancers. If her leader is a superior dancer, and dances at his highest level, then she may be forced to reveal her inexperience by misinterpretation and missteps. What's more, since the convention remains that men do the asking, even the most accomplished follower sometimes must endure the disappointment, if not humiliation, of not being asked to dance.

Another view of the dichotomy, though, can be argued more positively. An experienced couple we know eagerly shared with us their own hard won conclusion: The woman, in her submissive role, is really the more powerful in that her agreement to follow — to be submissive — is what makes the tango possible, and which leads, ideally, to the "tango moment," that sublime moment when leader and follower are in perfect balance and harmony.

Some elements of lead and follow are so subtle as to almost reverse the common explanation of male dominance, which results in a central enigma of tango — the less obvious but powerful role of the follower. The leader, after all, offers a lead, but it is up to the follower to take the time she needs to perform a response, thereby taking control momentarily of the pace and tempo. The worst mistake a leader can make, in my estimation, is to rush a follower. His role instead is to wait for the follower to complete her response to his lead before offering another lead. Although it may sound like a contradiction (tango is full of them) it's actually an example of where the woman's role is more active than passive.

Most of us women who have chosen partner dancing have come to pretty much accept our roles, no matter how submissive they seem to an outsider, and enjoy them. Then there are an adventurous few—perhaps in the American spirit of democracy, novelty, and equal opportunity—who practice the exchange of lead and follow; that is, in the midst of dancing, the woman and man reverse their arm positions, she then taking the lead and the man following. It is extraordinary to watch how smoothly some couples accomplish the exchange, without missing a beat, literally.

From whatever viewpoint you choose about dominance and submission, the basic requirements of lead and follow are pretty well agreed upon. First, both dancers are focused on maintaining their own axes. If they were to let go of one another at the *cruzada* (the cross) or almost anywhere, neither would fall over. In addition to both being on axis, the man's job is always to know where the woman's feet and weight are. The woman's job is to stay totally responsive to his signals about when to stay, when to move, and where to move. There are endless discussions, of course, about whose job is the more challenging. The leader sometimes complains of having so much responsibility—not only to decide which step or figure to lead but first to remember how to do it! (Gavito is known to say "never go for the step, go for the music.") And it's his job to navigate the floor, no matter how tall his partner or how big her hair. The follower, on the other hand, complains about how she must adapt from leader to leader, no matter how different their styles and ability levels.

Of course, a dancer's perceptions of his or her role will alter over time and increased skill. After two years of studying tango, my husband and I reported different degrees of satisfaction. His experiences leading advanced followers seemed more satisfying than mine as a follower dancing with advanced leaders. The reason wasn't clear at first, but is now: The chances were greater that any accomplished follower (with more experience than I had at the time) was going to be able to follow the leads he offered, while I was not always able to follow the leads a more accomplished leader offered me. That leader's repertory of leads, for example, might simply not have been familiar to me, or he may have led more subtly than I was used to.

After four years or so of experience, we witnessed still another shift. He became fearful of not being up to the challenge that sophisticated followers expected of him, while I was delighted to be invited to dance by an advanced leader and proud when I was able to follow respectably well. Over the last year, our moods and self-images altered almost daily. We seemed to be taking turns feeling satisfied with ourselves. Now, in our fifth year, we have reached a pleasurable plateau. Both of us confidently anticipate dancing with pros and also enjoy dancing with each other more than ever.

Leading with confidence… and sensitivity

Not long ago we were visited by some tango buddies we had met at an East Coast camp; our time with Mike and Angela felt like a week-long *practica,* considering how we spent every evening with a rolled up rug and a stack of tango CD's. Time not spent dancing was spent in conversation about tango, all of us marveling over the hold it has on our imaginations and priorities. Mike and Angela are spending their retirement years traveling the "tango trail" across America going from one dance festival or camp to another, including an annual trip to Buenos Aires, returning home only long enough to water the plants and pay the bills. Their youthful energy and younger than actual looks they attribute to this dancing lifestyle. What's more they share their enthusiasm and advice generously with others; we are immensely grateful to be a stop on their trail. And having their demos and advice about lead and follow opened our eyes about some basic stuff we missed on our own.

Mike stressed good leading technique, and his demos showed that technique as attainable… for both of us. Stand tall, keep the head up, he said to both of us; okay to lower the eyes but not the head. Lowering the body by bending the knees usually means some specific lead and should therefore be used intentionally. For example, the leader signals he's about to begin the dance by lowering before stepping out. But before stepping out, the leader must be careful to calm and focus his partner's attention, to stand in embrace with her, coordinating their breathing, and shifting her weight gently onto the leg where he wants her weight. Thus they can begin truly together. I found his explanation to be intensively sensitive to the needs of a follower and was glad my own partner was there to glean it. Adding sensitivity to confidence, the other major quality of a successful lead, again seems the ideal combination.

Angela added a point, from her experience, about the kind of leading embrace she likes best. In her opinion the true *tanguero* uses a close embrace to "cradle" his partner. By cradling, he was not just cuddling his partner for comfort but also to control her steps enough to give her confidence in following and, incidentally something I hadn't considered earlier, to protect her from another couple possibly crashing into them. I was reminded of Gavito's similar description of the ideal lead, but hers had added authority for me, coming as it did from an experienced follower. And especially reported as it was, from her experience dancing in Buenos Aires, the ultimate source, the mother country.

Following with sensitivity… and confidence

While they were visiting us, Mike and Angela attended our weekly local *practica*. Their enthusiasm about doing this, even after we explained that our friends were mostly beginners, surprised us at the time. Now that we've met other such generous dancers, we're beginning to understand the typical *tanguero* desire to help others catch the fever. After dancing with every one of our followers, Mike offered a diagnosis of their major need. He observed that what they all had in common was when they were led to step back, they moved the whole body back rather than just the leg, thereby losing their axis and pulling the leader forward and off his axis. Very bad form, this. We made a mental note to coach our followers on this point.

Later, it occurred to me that it might be every follower's first challenge that accounts for the beginner's awkward trouble with balance in the embrace—and that is the challenge of learning to dance, even walk, in high heeled shoes. Most women, even those who haven't worn them since their bra-burning days, really want the glam effect of strappy high heels. These women go through a period of painful adjustment; even American businesswomen tend not to wear high heels in normal life. So until they adjust to their shoes, their feet ache, their ankles wobble, their knees buckle, their calves cramp. In most cases, progression in the dance parallels adjustment to the shoes one wants to wear. Some women give up, though, and simply wear dance sneakers with pants, even to milongas; others make do with low sensible heels

Overall, the most useful advice Mike gave to our followers was what I had heard so many teachers say again and again: aim to be as light and responsive to your partner as humanly possible; that means keeping your balance (body weight) over your axis, so that if your partner were to stop and let go of you—at any point in the dance—you would not fall over, but instead be able to stand alone on whichever foot you had been placed. A tall order, he agreed, acknowledging our nervous laughter, but "it is what we should be working toward if we want to become beautiful dancers. All the *maestros* we've met say this."

Still, he was quick to add a footnote to temper any impression we may have received about the follower's apparent submissiveness in all this. (For me, it was an echo of what I had already discovered on my own.) "Remember," he urged us, "it is the follower who ultimately controls the tempo across the floor because she can take whatever time she needs to complete a figure." In other words, she should be poised and waiting for a lead, and avoid anticipating, but the leader must give her the time to complete it and thus slow down the dance at her command.

The Style Factor

Those who haven't yet been to Buenos Aires are told to be prepared for some differences on the dance floors there. The major one is about style. On crowded floors there, we were told and then found it to be true, you can expect everyone to be dancing "*milonguero* style," also known here as club style or close embrace style. This style danced close with small steps confines itself to a limited vocabulary of steps—many of them abbreviated versions of classical steps—to create an economy of movement and space required for execution. For example, classical front *ochos* (fan-like pivots that are signature steps of the tango) are reduced to *ochos cortados,* in which the follower is taken outside partner for half an *ocho* and then returned to the chest-to-chest position by the leader. Back *ochos* are performed similarly, without the usual hip twist but rather a simple diagonal cross of one foot behind the other as the leader continues in "cross system" (leader's right foot steps concurrent with follower's right foot rather than the more common "parallel system" where leader's left foot steps with the follower's right) so that partners can remain glued together. It could be regarded as a variation that began as a practical accommodation but which evolved into a distinct style. West Coast swing comes to mind, also an accommodation of space-demanding East Coast Swing to crowded West Coast dance floors, thus evolving into a distinctive style, one that offers highly syncopated movement in a narrow slot of space. The music that most often inspires *milonguero* style dancing is that with a steady, semi-quick beat from the classical 40's repertory.

While the more open "salon style" with its large and unrestrained vocabulary of steps, considered classical to many, may be danced where space is not an issue in Buenos Aires, it is never led there alternately with *milonguero* style in a given dance to one piece of music. Here in the U.S., however, a leader may start a dance in *milonguero* style, then open up to salon style in order to lead a more complex figure, especially if the music changes tempo as it often does, and then return to close embrace. In Buenos Aires it is a matter of respecting the purity and consistency of a style, we're told.

Another tango style that we are seeing more of, especially among younger *tangueros* on the West Coast, is what is increasingly referred to as *Tango Nuevo* or "New Generation Tango." The delightful Fabian Salas, who played one of Sally Potter's coaches in "The Tango Lesson," reveals a hint of this style in the film, but we didn't see it as distinctive until we had experienced several group lessons with him, first at Nora's Week, then at Miami Tango Fantasy. In this style, the leader's steps are large and ambling and highly syncopated to match syncopated music, the leading hand held low, the embrace open and loose, the leader's knees more often than not bent and ready to spring. The first time I was led in this style, my partner apologized laughingly for being so "hoppy," but he had clearly enjoyed himself, and I felt exhilarated by the speed of our trajectory across the floor. When I caught my breath, I noticed that New Generation, like its youthful adherents, suggests a "costume:" for the man, athletic shoes, baggy pants usually cargo pants, a dress shirt worn as a casual open jacket over a tee shirt; optional spiked hair. For the woman it's low slung, skin tight dance pants, high heels or dance sneakers, and brief, cleavage-swelling top. It's clearly a street-wise and post-modern alternative to the elegance of salon style tango.

Included in the larger tango genre (that also embraces New Generation styles) are two distinct and important relatives of tango, both evolving from folk dances and folk rhythms, and both danced at milongas in response to specific music. One is tango *vals* or waltz, also called *vals criolla,* the other known simply as *milonga.* Tango waltz is often interpreted simply as dancing tango steps to 3/4 time, at its fastest tempos stepping only on beat one. Teachers of group classes in tango waltz, though, usually include some steps specifically evolved or designed to take unique advantage of waltz tempo. The same goes for *milonga* which, with its quick and small staccato steps—one for each beat of the music—and its bouncy rhythm, looks to some observers like "cowboy tango" or a Latino version of the Texas two step, also influenced by European polka. Adding a playful *milonga* rhythm into the tango mix of music at a *milonga* is like injecting some comic relief into a serious drama. We are reminded of merengue by the pulse and buoyant atmosphere of the *milonga* variety. (Larry calls *milonga* "the one tango style that you can smile broadly through and not look silly.")

The multiplicity of styles that make up subsets of Argentine tango allows for wonderfully diverse interpretations of tango tempos and rhythms. But it also adds to the complexity of learning tango and may frustrate any learner, especially the reluctant learner. The couple you're about to meet in the next story struggle with the fact that he doesn't find tango all that pleasurable, while she finds not only pleasure in it but success in the learning of it. There may be no easy answer to this dilemma, or is there?

"Dedication Required"

a story

ALVIN PAUSED in flossing between the upper right and lower right teeth. As his wife dabbed the make-up off her eyes he asked, "Didn't you think that was an odd statement to make at a first dance class?"

"The part about having to make regular pilgrimages to the city to learn tango well?" Frannie glanced over with her naked eye and then looked back to the mirror to strip off the painted adornments on the other one.

Alvin took note of which molar he was on before stopping to answer. "Not so much that one, though I guess they're related. The one that got me was that at the end of this four week series, this "introductory, barely scratching the surface" set of classes, we still won't know enough to really be dancing tango."

"I think they're just warning us so we won't get discouraged."

"What about now? It's like being told don't bother with this jogging class if you're not going to run a marathon." His wife leaned over the sink and Alvin watched as her breasts grazed lightly on the edge of the counter and her skirt tightened against the firm bottom of a thirty-seven year old.

"I don't think that's what they mean." Frannie rinsed her face, patted at the water with a towel and blinked at her husband through short lashes. "They're just letting us know that the tango is a complicated dance and there's no short cut to learning it. This one class won't be enough, that's all."

Alvin spat the toothpaste out in the sink and sloshed water to clean it up, smearing the bits of mascara that had landed on the porcelain. It wasn't his job to clean them up. The biting odor of chemical solvent grabbed the back of his throat. "Couldn't you have waited to do your nails until I was done in here?"

"Sorry. There's no time in the morning and several are chipped."

Alvin left the bathroom and removed the stacks of pillows from the bed. Drowsiness replaced irritation. He was startled awake by Frannie bouncing into bed fifteen minutes later. She leaned into him with cold hands and said, "Thanks for taking the classes with me. I think it's going to be great fun." Frannie settled her naked belly and chest against his side. She was wide-awake and would try to please him now, if he wanted. Alvin quietly considered making love to his wife and reaping the rewards of going along with her new passion, but it was late and his body seemed to have taken a head start towards rest.

Ready with a handful of steps from completing the first four-week series of tango and protected by the companionship of the other, Alvin and Frannie entered the club and stopped by the door. A score of couples embraced on a crowded floor slipping their legs into their partner's space as if to threaten, only to caress.

Frannie's grip tightened on his arm as Alvin said, "We're not even in the same league as anyone out there."

"The teachers said that a lot of beginners come here on Thursday."

"They must be the ones sitting down." All of the empty chairs held coats or faced a table with unfinished beverages. Frannie and Alvin stood behind a row of unoccupied chairs for several songs.

"We might as well try dancing," she offered. Adding their coats to a pile, they stepped onto the floor.

"Let's just not crash into anybody," Alvin said and began an eight-count pattern. Completing it once, he started it again. Before they could finish, a couple swerved in front of them and Alvin stopped in the middle. He sensed someone off his right side starting to pass them. Forgetting where he was in the pattern, he tried a simple walk. Frannie's weight was on the other foot and they stumbled, not enough to fall, but it wasn't pretty. They silently regrouped, a stalled vehicle on a busy boulevard. Alvin checked the traffic and started them walking again. Dancing couples darted at them like bats at dusk in a cloud of insects, catching their meal before swerving at the last instant to avoid the lumbering spectacle of the beginner couple. Accomplishing little more than walking in a semblance of tango rhythm, they lasted the song and exited quickly to some chairs that held only coats.

They sat in silence through the next song. In the short break between numbers he leaned over and whispered in her ear, "That was hell."

Without looking at him Frannie said, "We just need more practice."

A few days later, Alvin and Frannie sat in a restaurant booth across from two longtime friends. "Tango! It sounds so romantic." Celeste spoke like she was making an announcement. She was settled against Gus who nodded in agreement. Alvin knew Gus's look; it meant, affirm her enthusiasm, but don't encourage her or I'll end up in the class, too. Alvin and Gus had worked at the same office for nearly twenty years. They had bonded around their respective divorce proceedings soon after they met. Alvin had married Frannie a couple years later, but Gus had remained single, having had few relationships which lasted more than a year. Celeste was only the second to move in with him. Alvin could go along with Celeste's zeal and gain a scrap of admiration from his friend's voluptuous girlfriend, but he knew he didn't have the acting ability to pull it off. Instead he answered, "All it is is difficult right now."

"The first thing the teachers did was warn us that it takes a long time to learn," Frannie responded, starting her statement looking at Alvin and then turning towards their friends when Alvin looked over. "I'd like to continue taking classes and give it a real try." She glanced back at Alvin. He hadn't agreed to this yet.

"It sounds like such fun!" Celeste had one arm wrapped around Gus's neck. "We should tango sometime."

"Yeah," Gus forced enthusiasm to the front of his mouth. "Maybe next year when the remodel is done."

Alvin concluded that what Frannie really wanted was the flame of romance, reminiscent of the blaze they had in their early years together, which now had become little more than the dim glow of a night light. He picked her up from her job and took her out to dinner and a movie in Healdsburg in the middle of the week, something they hadn't managed in a year or so. Afterwards they made love. The caressing and mutual pleasuring was enjoyable, if still predictable. On the weekend he brought her a bouquet.

His attempt to replace Frannie's desire for tango backfired. As they drove south for the last class of the current series she said, "Don't you think we've been more romantic with each other since we've started tangoing?"

"Maybe it's because we started talking about it."

"But I still think tango was one of the main reasons we've been talking about…" and here she slowed and pronounced the next words as if they needed testing, "…our love life." Alvin felt the familiar weight from bearing the load of a partner's disappointment; he felt it settle somewhere inside his chest and pinch the muscles across his shoulders. Frannie spoke again, interrupting the drone of the tires on the freeway. "I'd like us to take classes in Marin next and go to a dance one other night of the week."

"I believe the psychological term for what you're going through is obsession."

"What? If I like something a lot then it's considered unhealthy?"

"I didn't say unhealthy."

"But that's what you mean by 'obsession,' isn't it? That I'm doing something that isn't smart?"

"What is so compelling about dancing tango?" Alvin asked.

Frannie turned her head towards the side window, folded her arms and opened them again. She said, "When I'm tangoing, it feels like my life is complete. Like there's nothing better that could be happening. I suppose that doesn't make any sense to you."

"You think I might feel that way if I was better at it?"

"I don't know if you will. But I do want us to share the tango together. Like they said, it's harder for a leader in the beginning."

Alvin and Frannie drove down to San Francisco for a Sunday tango workshop given by a visiting Argentine couple. They had just finished their third set of classes the preceding week and were encouraged to try the pair of two-hour workshops with famous visiting Argentine masters.

The class was taken through several walking warm-ups via the use of a translator from the teacher's native Spanish to English. Then the teachers whisked through a pattern of steps a few times and invited the class to try it.

Alvin gave Frannie an exaggerated blink and said, "I guess you know what we're supposed to do?"

"That wasn't much of an explanation. Let's watch someone else."

They looked around and saw the reign of confusion. So did the teachers who called attention back to the center. They demonstrated the pattern of steps twice at full speed and then a third time following the spontaneous requests of several students.

Alvin repeated the exercise of failure. He could barely keep track of his own feet, much less Frannie's. The teachers toured the room giving hands-on assistance for twenty minutes, demonstrated again, and worked individually with each student. The female instructor granted Alvin a large dose of personal attention, walking him through every step while he teetered and stumbled. The male teacher gave them time as well, steering Frannie through the whole pattern on the third try. In his limited English he attempted to direct Alvin, but soon parted with a quick word of encouragement.

"He knows hopeless when he sees it," Alvin said.

"That's not true. This is just more advanced than anything we've tried so far."

Alvin and Frannie ignored the first call for a partner change. On the second one, Frannie asked if he would mind if they tried it with someone different. He started to object, but she said, "Just see how it goes" and walked to the next guy. His new partner was soon trying to teach him. It was English and the words were recognizable, only the vocabulary was of a language he didn't know. He apologized. She encouraged him. They stood and watched other couples. They changed partners again and Alvin stepped out of the circle and took a seat, explaining briefly to his would-be partner that he was lost and not up to this level. He saw everyone else dancing through the pattern, though he had no idea whether any of the couples he watched were dancing it correctly. Frannie was smiling.

During the lunch break between classes Alvin informed Frannie that he had had enough for the day, but since they had paid in advance, she should take the class and he'd walk around for a couple of hours. She protested at first, then acquiesced once it was clear that he wasn't asking her to leave.

Alvin found a bar a couple blocks away from the ballroom. The Giants were playing on a big screen TV. He took a stool at the bar, ordered an Anchor Steam and dropped into the game.

"Think the Giants are going to make the playoffs?" the woman on the stool behind him asked. She was in her forties, tall, with a smoker's sultry tone and enough nicotine to keep her thin. She was a natural blond beauty, employing modern assistance to maintain her gifts. Her blue eyes glistened as she opened them to their full potential.

"I don't know. I don't keep track like I used to."

"You didn't come here for the game?"

"No. I was down the street at a tango workshop." He hesitated. "My wife's still there, but I've had enough of it. I'm afraid she likes it a whole lot more than I do."

"Tango. Roses in your teeth and all that stuff?"

"I guess. It's suppose to be fun but you can't take a step without holding your body just so and twisting like you don't really want to go there."

"I like simpler things myself." She tilted her head back and sipped on her Margarita. The sparse buttons of her tightly stretched blouse allowed a glimpse of ample breasts. She sucked momentarily on a large ice cube before dropping it back in the glass. As she returned her gaze, he was watching a drop of water run over her red lower lip and down her chin. She dabbed it off with her finger and wiped it on the soft indentation at the base of her neck.

"I'm Jolene."

"Al. Do you live around here?"

"Walking distance. What about you?"

"Cloverdale."

"You came all this way for a dance class? Your wife must really like it."

"Some people commute daily to work in San Francisco from Cloverdale."

A roar emanated from the screen and several people in the bar whooped in unison. The batter had rounded first base and took second standing. "Finally the Giants have a guy on base," Jolene said, keeping her eyes on the screen. Alvin liked it when she talked so he had an excuse to look at her.

"So, Jolene, are you a big baseball fan?"

"I just like the Giants."

"Do you like…"

"Shh…" She took his upper arm and turned him towards the screen. Leaning close enough that he could feel her breath, smoky tequila, she said, "Let's see if the next batter can bring him home." Jolene kept her right hand on his arm and leaned her left arm on the bar as she peered past his shoulder to the drama of baseball.

The Giants left the runner stranded on second. Neither team scored in the next inning. He learned that Jolene was the office manager for a civil engineering firm and had a nineteen-year-old away at college. He also wanted to know what it would be like to place his hand on her bare thigh.

The Giants lost. The tango class would be over in ten minutes. Alvin had drunk two beers and wanted a third, which he didn't order. Jolene plied him with questions and let her eyes drift over his whole face as he talked, frequently watching the words come out of his lips while she moistened her own.

"Well, I've got to get back to the dance studio," Alvin said. "I've enjoyed watching the game with you, Jolene."

"Me too." She stood up when he did. "Maybe we'll meet for another game sometime?" Jolene held out her hand. As he took her hand, he knew that she would say yes to other things, things that proceeded by instinct and were mysterious only in their existence and not in their execution. They would also make his life very complex.

When Alvin got back to the studio, it was half empty. Frannie was practicing a step with a fellow student. She was pressed tight against him while he repeatedly slipped one leg and then another between hers. He wished for a moment that he had given Jolene a parting hug as an antidote to what he now felt. When Frannie saw Alvin, she finished the pattern with her partner, thanked him and jogged over to her husband. "I wish you would have been here. They kept working from the same pattern and people were getting it by the end." How pretty his wife was, he thought, and felt the gnawing feeling in his stomach of having disappointed her again. He wondered though, if she might have had a better time without him. "What did you do?" she asked.

"Not much. I watched a baseball game in a bar."

"I thought you were tired of baseball."

"I am, but I was in the mood for something simple."

Chapter 3

The Challenge

Learning It: A Dancer's History

IT'S A STRANGE process, learning to tango. Some call it adventure because when you set out you never really know where you're going. And as we've stressed before, it doesn't happen quickly, this acquisition of tango. What must happen, before anything else can be set into motion, is that you must fall in love with the music. If tango music doesn't make your heart race, if it doesn't make you want to "be" with it, then chances are tango will never become your passion. And without passion, unfortunately, progress is slow, maybe even non-existent. For us, the very first exposure to *La Cumparsita* played by a tango orchestra fueled our passion toward dancing to that music.

At the start, we watched the pros, usually show dancers in some flashy, fleshy film or exhibition; flying legs, alternating with bundled legs, glittering under the lights, quick complex connections between the dancers, the obvious passion, solemn faces full of longing. "We want to do that!" we cried, leaving the theater panting, eyes wide. While we were so moved and exhilarated by what we heard and saw, we simultaneously feared it as the unknown and maybe even the unknowable. And so what better to do than make fun of ourselves; we played tango in bed, snappily wrapping and unwrapping our legs around each others, kicking and laughing playfully at our parody. Secretly, at first anyway, we each in our own way longed to dance it for real. And it was that longing that marked the beginning of our tango odyssey. Our new tango friends would all tell remarkably similar stories.

It may take two to tango but it takes only one to arrange for a lesson, or in our case, push the other one in making that first step. Frank had earlier resisted my requests to try the one tango class we had heard about in our area. He had argued—petulantly, I thought at the time—that we were still learning other ballroom dances and had plenty to learn with those. Why try to add another dance to the mix? Finally desperate, I decided to put him on the spot. I asked for a private tango lesson for my birthday. Petulance put aside and seeing I was serious, he agreed, marking the official onset of our mad journey into Argentine tango.

Our fine first teachers taught both group and private lessons, but we lived too far away to take regular group lessons. Besides, we knew that private lessons would give us the kind of introduction we needed, one that would show us if tango was a dance we were capable of. They began slowly with us, much slower than we expected; our first two-hour lesson consisted of walking, marking time for a simple turn (*cadenza*) and the basic eight step pattern. (Today, more often than not, teachers don't begin with any "basic" pattern, but rather teach people to improvise within the principles of walking together.)

We were not to return until we had perfected these simple steps our teachers insisted... kindly but seriously.

To this day, we often retell this story—with appropriate awe for our first teachers—to beginning students. In retrospect we see how wise they were to dismiss our illusions; instead of giving us what we thought we wanted—quick and easy, but intricate footwork—they forced us to focus on the basics. We are infinitely grateful for their restraint and wisdom, based no doubt on their experience of teaching tango to others like us who, in all ignorance, wanted fast results. For example, at our first lesson, they demonstrated simple *ochos* (figure eights) and we, unimpressed, asked about *ganchos* (lightning fast leg hooks). Unfazed, no doubt amused, they waved away any thoughts of *ganchos*, or *ochos* for that matter, and sent us on our way to practice walking, walking, walking in the tango manner. Properly chastened, we did just that, coming to appreciate fully, on our own living room floor, what a challenging set of skills we had so blithely taken on.

We know now how right our teachers were. Tango students who want to *gancho* before they walk may never get tango at all, for the stylized walking-in-embrace that forms the foundation of tango's figures, when done correctly, makes possible everything else that's beautiful about tango. The tango walk, unlike walking normally, requires intense concentration at first. No wonder its list of component parts reads like a technical manual! Moving together, partners must slide the traveling foot along the floor, toe first, immediately in front (or back) of the weight-bearing foot allowing the thighs to brush in the process, transfer weight, and bring the traveling foot to brush against the weight-bearing foot while completing the step. The feet then, in walking, never leave the floor; one foot is carrying the weight, the other moves while caressing the floor. The leg as it reaches out forward or backward is straight until it accepts some weight at which point the knee "softens," or bends slightly to accept the full weight, but smoothly.

Not surprisingly, tango walk takes some self-conscious practice, preferably in front of a mirrored wall. When we were no longer embarrassed about our walk, and felt we were "presentable" to our teachers, we returned to them for evaluation. Thrilled to have passed scrutiny, we were accepted for a second lesson that included front and back *ochos*. We were on our way, or so we thought.

The next step for us was to sample group lessons, both cheaper and less intensive than privates. Ideally, having a regular weekly lesson is the way most people start seriously, but we lived in rural northern California far from a large-sized town. We could attend classes in the nearest city only sporadically. So we turned to videos. Then we braved a milonga or two, one hosted by our first teachers, another by one of the dance clubs in San Francisco.

We've since discovered that our experiences during the next stage of tango acquisition were not at all unique to us. Smiles of familiarity greet us whenever we share some embarrassing memories of early milongas. There we were, fully aware of our limitations as beginners, sitting out the first few sets to watch the more experienced dancers, admiringly, longingly. Eager to try out what we've learned, we gather our courage to get out on the floor. But what's wrong? We'd gotten a nod on that step or figure from a teacher, but now we couldn't do it on the milonga floor! Not with each other, not with anyone else. We leave frustrated, angry at ourselves for what looks like regression. What's going on? Maybe it's just too much for us.

The Confidence Factor

There are plenty of ironies to face (and enjoy) when learning to tango, but the major one is this: you have to regress and be thoroughly humbled in order to go forward. Classic American impatience doesn't help, of course. And you have to want it enough to push through the despair barrier. It is the recurring feeling that something is wrong that impels the potential dancer to go forward. Many give up at this point. It may be that they just don't want it enough, or they are willing to settle for advanced mediocrity. Those who go forward do it because they are determined to become confident enough to "get it." That eventuality indeed requires the ironic fact that confidence comes before accomplishment. It takes confidence to keep returning to the basics without feeling diminished. It takes confidence to be willing to put in the time for practicing the basics as well as for dancing socially for fun. The basics are hard: weight, balance, axis, embrace, hand-hold, the walk, walk, walk that every class and *practica* begins with. The basics are, one discovers, again ironically—harder to perfect than the advanced figures. You have to let go of some ego to accept the steep learning curve of tango. At the same time, you have to be confident enough to accept that after a few years you may still not be squarely in the Intermediate class.

Once there is confidence (which may be defined as the certainty that you WILL improve with time, not that you've already gotten there), there is some relaxation. Then the learner can move from his brain (imagining tango) and body (steps and figures) to his heart (feeling and intimacy and oneness). Making the body do the right things, though, and doing those things compatibly and in harmony with another person is the next hurdle.

Why is tango so difficult to learn? A question that may precede this one is "how much time are you willing to commit?" Tango may not require the number of hours it takes to learn jazz piano or classical guitar, but it's close. In fact many people claim it helps to approach tango as if it were learning a musical instrument. As Larry says, "Tango doesn't give up its secrets easily. Can your ego take it? Nowhere in dance do students retake beginning level classes the way they do in tango. People who eventually progress in tango are those who have stopped feeling diminished by taking still another beginner's lesson."

Larry reports his experience as a leader this way: "I must have taken twenty beginner's lessons, but they still hold value for me. And just when I'm sure I'm leading a step just as I've been taught, someone comes along who has been taught (equally correctly) to do it a different way. Can I then be secure enough in myself to adapt my hard obtained skills in order to make my partner happy that she danced with me? One of the great beauties of tango is its ability to allow for the personal signature of every dancer. A wonderful attribute of the tango, yes, but it will require even more patience from you to allow for the individual expression of your follower. You won't have this problem learning International foxtrot, that's for sure, but then again you don't get to improvise in International foxtrot either."

Improvisation

The improvisation factor in tango is one of its challenges but also one of its greatest rewards. Unlike in other ballroom dances, there is no one correct way to execute a step in tango, that is, there is no ideal form to which every dancer aspires. There is not even a rule about dancing to the tempo of the music since the leader may pause whenever he wishes. There are categories of figures such as *salidas* (entrance steps), walking steps, *giros* (turning patterns where the man is like the hub and the woman the wheel moving around him), and *firuletes,* adornments that everyone learns, but they are subject to as many variations as there are dancers. Once a leader acquires even a small "vocabulary" of steps, and a basic "grammar" of figures and styles, he's in a position to dance creatively to the music, freely drawing on his vocabulary and grammar to make every dance a unique expression of that music. The important factor is how well the steps are led and how smoothly followed. His follower, if she is prepared to follow sensitively, will be adding wind to their sails as they glide across the floor in a way neither may have ever done before.

We fully came to know the role of improvisation in our own pleasure of tango when we were asked to do a performance at a local benefit event. My husband's hesitation to accept the invitation irked me; why not give it a try? No one in our small town expects us to be pros. Besides, I argued, it would be a chance to introduce people to salon tango as a contrast to what they think tango is — showy stage tango, with the leader lifting his partner over his head, clearly what we *wouldn't* be doing. He finally relented, but as we rehearsed for the performance, I came to understand what he objected to most: having to plan and choreograph our steps. Where we usually and happily have no idea how and where any one dance will go, where each dance to the same piece of music is never danced the same way twice, my partner, now fearing his brain would fail him by forgetting every lead he ever knew, was now struggling to match steps in advance to a piece of music we were replaying ad nauseam, having to create mnemonic devices to remember them. He hated the process; he much preferred the approach to tango we were taught at our first lesson, which was to dance for one another, for himself and his partner, for no one else, and dancing so harmoniously as to hear each other's heartbeat.

Settings for learning Tango

Private lessons, regular group lessons, weekend workshops, milongas, camps, and festivals. Where is the best place for the novice to start? To some degree, this decision depends on where you live. If you're far from a city and can't attend a weekly group class, the best place to get started is by taking a few monthly private lessons from a reputable teacher. Check for web sites of the tango activity in your area and for reputable teachers by searching under: <u>Tango+ name of city or state.</u> If you live in or near a big city, besides checking web sites you can also check the yellow pages for ballroom dance studios, whose staff can help you find local tango teachers or group lessons.

The advantage of group lessons for beginners is the lower stress, cost, and perhaps intimidation level, as compared to private lessons. New dancers as a group can support and commiserate with one another, urge one another to keep trying, inject some humor, and provide a social setting for making new friends. "Dance buddies" make great friends, we've found. Lessons go like this: the teacher usually leads a warm-up exercise across the floor. Then he or she demonstrates the step or feature to be taught at that lesson. Students practice the step with the nearest partner, then switch partners to practice again. Teachers usually have a strategy for partner-changing to make it happen smoothly and without awkwardness because they strongly believe that the more partners the better, even when some couples are mismatched. The end of a group lesson usually makes way for some open practice, and occasionally—maybe once a month—the teacher will host a dance party (milonga) where students can dress up and get a taste of tango as it is danced, rather than only as it is "practiced."

One of the most influential *tangueras* ever, Susana Miller, rates milongas as primary to the tango experience. "I think the *tanguedad* ("tango-ness") of the tango is in the party. If there are no parties there is no *tanguedad* in tango."

Another way to make progress in tango is to pack up and attend a "tango camp." Like other adult camps, these are intense affairs involving several days, or even a week, of dancing with *maestros* and other students all day in workshops, then dancing at a milonga most of the night. Older dancers like us usually have to take some breaks and pace ourselves in order to keep up. Fortuitously, we also have to leave the milongas early, which gives me some downtime to record impressions in my journal.

Dance Camp: Some Recollections

Nora's Tango Week 2000. Nora of "Nora's Week" is Nora Dinzelbacher, an unusual name for a Latina, one might think, but not for a *tanguera* from Argentina. (Remember how diverse Argentina's original population was.) Nora is very well-known as a teacher in San Francisco. We are admirers of her and her sassy, slightly pushy, but always clear teaching style. She works especially well with men, communicating their responsibility to them better than most teachers, and without bruising egos.

The night before leaving. Anticipation. Jitters. We haven't danced enough lately and so both of us feel unready. We've given up the monthly trips to the city for dancing in favor of domestic chores and local commitments. Feeling stiff as we do reminds us of our ages and of the demands of tango... to make progress one must dance regularly if the muscles are to make memories and retain them.

I'm awake at 4 A.M. the morning we're to leave. Last night Frank had the sneezes and a toothache. Is this anxiety too? I'm anxious about the levels... are we high intermediates or low advanced? Should we change partners or stick together? I sense a new determination to feel confident enough to be cool. Have expectations of my partners. Avoid apologizing for a misstep... assume it was the leader's fault, as it no doubt is, according to some teachers who argue that any mistake is due to a mislead. How comforting if true. Should I pretend I know what I'm doing and thereby regulate my cool and confidence? Creating awe among the less skilled? Ahhhh, fantasy.

Did I bring the right clothes? I woke up this morning imagining an outfit I had packed, then realized no dance shoes would go with it, so I must replace some part of it. Bringing entirely too much, I fear, but what if I tear something or dirty something? Having the right clothes and shoes are so much a part of the experience — for both comfort and style. Last night's packing frenzy was disturbing to remember, poised in front of my closet, seriously contemplating each possibility. Too dressy? Too warm? Too fragile? A large suitcase was already full, and I was still adding to it, subtracting from it. An occasional wave of reality therapy is tapped: you're 60 years old. You're no longer thin. You're no one's sexual object beyond your husband's appreciative attention; it doesn't matter whom you impress or fail to; you've already proven plenty by just getting out on the floor and going out of your way to attend this thing. Relax, relax, relax.

July 11. We slept through our first class. Refreshed at last, so that the second class was do-able. In fact I was peppier than the rest and impatient with the slow pace. Even walked to the local deli for lunch.

"Progressive tango" is what we just experienced, a new teaching strategy for us. All attendees and teachers gather in one large room. Each set of teachers demonstrates a pattern for five minutes, then we practice it for fifteen minutes or so. The next pair of teachers demonstrates something that builds on what came before.

I am talking too much during the lessons, I see from reactions from others, including Frank, who suggests that I don't ask questions casually. We meet our former West Coast Swing teachers who are now in beginner's class. A rush, a refreshing reversal of being advanced over them and wanting to encourage them to stay with it.

After dinner, relaxing in our room, we watch the video tape Frank took of last night's "Dream Team" performances. (It's customary for the teachers at a camp to do a brief performance on opening night). Nora announces, for the record: "look at them, you'll never see all of them together like this, the best tango teachers who have ever come to the U.S., a dream team." She may very well be right... we've heard of all these dancers, read about their international reputations, seen some of them perform in "Forever Tango" on stage or in "The

Tango Lesson." All of them strikingly attractive, glamorously attired, whatever their ages: Gavito and Marcela, Nito and Elba, Juan Carlos Copes and daughter Johanna, Fabian and Carolina, Fernanda and Guillermo, Eduardo and Gloria.

We catch them briefly on tape admiring each other at the Teachers Table, after each performance effusively sharing kisses and embraces; colleagues, *compadres,* hallowed members of Los *Maestros* club calling out *"eso, eso!"* after a particularly well-executed figure. Today's headlines about Argentina's economic crisis pass ironically before my eyes. While Argentina burns, its international loans not being repaid and therefore inciting an economic crash, a few Argentinos are dancing on the international scene for big money. Coming the full circle, really, considering the origins of tango in the alleyways of *el conventillo,* danced by *los pobrecitos* and petty criminals to forget their troubles. But who could deny them their glamorous trappings, no matter how ironic? They represent perhaps the best, most enduring, part of their national culture.

Later that night, maybe 3 AM, we are awakened by noisy lovers in next room, their wall-penetrating moaning punctuated by crescendos and decrescendos of panting. Lying awake together, we pick out a tango beat underlying the percussion and have to stifle our laughter. It's tango for sure that's behind this unexpected performance. Now, which couple might this be? We speculate wildly. Could it be one of the *maestro* couples? No, they are housed in suites on another floor. But maybe some of the assistants? One thing for sure... this couple has tango deeply embedded in their lives to have enough energy — and inspiration — for lovemaking at this hour.

July 15. Dreams. Frank's and mine are similar. Someone is teaching him something but placing obstacles deliberately in his path; I'm being victimized by a group, shunned, cast out of a class of some sort. We're aware, when we discuss our dreams that our level of confidence must still be low. What I'm sure of is that I'm consistently intimidated by my partners, even when they are not as experienced or skilled as I. Wanting desperately to be considered a good partner, I tense up, freeze, miss even the simplest leads. The question for me is whether I should continue with group lessons where partners must be changed. Is it still tango if I dance only with my husband?

Portland Tango Fest Oct 2001 This feels good. There is a friendliness and sort of down-home quality to the Portland scene, yet without losing its mystical worship of tango and its appeal to us the faithful. Maybe because it's designed and staffed mostly by American teachers rather than Argentines. Excellent professional teachers from around the country who have studied with Argentines, but because they are Americans they understand the peculiarly American psyche: our problem acquiring confidence, our sexual issues, our need for breaking down the figures into steps. Meanwhile, the few Argentines who *are* here are wonderfully accessible: the young and beautiful Miriam and Hugo from "Forever Tango" and the comically casual *"El Pulpo"* (the octopus) who seems to grow extra legs as he winds his two through his partner's in the pursuit of continuous *ganchos*. He is also known to tango to rock and roll music.

There are several teachers here who focus on "close embrace" style (also called *"milonguero style"* or "club style") which is a really nice addition for us since that style is so popular in San Francisco milongas, yet rarely taught at workshops. This is the style done chest to chest with all the action in the legs—small steps, syncopations. We'll need to do some private lessons in this style because even excellent group instruction is so limited. We've met one couple we could study with, the very distinctive Christopher and Caroline, based in Marin County, only three hours away from us, if we can ever get our tango travel trip together. How I wish Frank were already retired.

Last set of classes, last day of the festival. My feet are swollen, my knees are beginning to buckle. I snapped at the last partner I had, and he shot me a surprised and hurt look. It's time. I give up and go back to the hotel planning to nap, but sleep won't come. This is just too much. What am I thinking to put myself through this agony? I'm too old for this. Frank thinks I'm a wuss—I can see it on his face; our tango buddies aren't nearly as tired. But I have troubling joints and a history of back problems. Damn.

Seems to me I said all these things at the end of Nora's too. Maybe I shouldn't be so hard on myself. This is not an endurance test. Or is it?

After the last night's milonga...: I'm so glad I didn't miss it. A live tango orchestra at the Crystal Ballroom, Portland's most elegant venue, with architecture from the 30's and 40's era of the Big Band dance halls, and a perfectly sprung floor that encourages you to fly across it. I chose to wear my fringed long dress with the red and black ankle strap pumps, just dressy enough for this event. My feet suddenly don't hurt anymore. I hate leaving, I really do.

Miami Tango Fantasy May 2002 This one is different from both Nora's Week and the Portland Tango Fest. More international in flavor, Miami being after all the capital of Latin America and closer to the East Coast cities, worldliness is in the air we breathe around here at the Fountainbleau Hotel in Miami Beach. You hear New York and Boston accents everywhere, also lots of Spanish and occasional French and German. The interlude music between tango sets is Afro Cuban and the second favorite dance is salsa. A comic counterpoint not-to-be-missed in the lobbies and elevators are odd collections of hip-hoppers and their fans, in the midst of their own convention in this hotel. Our first reaction is "whoa, pimps and hookers on the make." And then when we find out the source, we simply laugh at the clash of fashion statements—when elaborate corn rows and day-glo athletic shoes meet slicked-back hair and stiletto heels—which were themselves, ironically enough, the look of pimps and hookers from another era.

Like the other camps, dance days are long and challenging; milongas tend to go on too long for our stamina. For all the dancers' sophistication here, they don't seem necessarily more skilled than West Coast dancers. Still, one difference I notice is that the teachers seem to attend all the milongas and dance with people other than their partners, so there must be a higher level of dancers here, or at least the perception of such.

One generalization is possible: there is more, and more elegant, salon style here in Miami, more close-embrace-club style in the West. I'm reminded once again of the difference between East Coast Swing and West Coast Swing dancing. At one evening's milonga, we notice a familiar couple on the floor. We had met them last fall at Portland. Reintroducing ourselves to each other made for a special evening since we exchanged partners and compared our experiences at both events.

The following night we see another set of familiar faces; these lovely people we had met at Nora's Week, Michael and Angela of Tampa Beach. Their invitation to join their table eventually led to our invitation to visit us on their next trip to California. That they took us up on the invitation showed us again how strong the "tango tie" can become, that when tango is the shared passion, two relative sets of strangers can become intimate friends in a few moments on a dance floor and beyond. This couple is the same Mike and Angela who danced with us in our living room and coached our home-grown tango buddies with so much generosity.

Portland Tango Fest, October 2002

October 16, day one. Seeing some familiar faces was a welcome way to begin this first afternoon of our third Portland experience, one that was otherwise disappointing. Sometimes it happens that way at a tango festival camp; we got more out of watching fifteen minutes of an advanced class on *sacadas* than from attending an intermediate class on club-style which we believed would be just right for us. It wasn't. The tedium of repeating a simple step ad nauseam with every dancer in the room was more than we could tolerate. Here it was the first day and my feet hurt already. So we crept upstairs, watched the instructor demonstrate a step so clearly that we "got" it pronto, just watching. Although it was too late to join that class, we had a friend video us performing the complicated figure at the end of the day so we could remember to try it at home. Maybe there was a positive side to this experience, we told each hopefully; maybe we were readier for advanced classes than we thought? We are also reminded about how useful it is to bring a video camera to tango camps.

Day two. There's no denying it, this was a watershed day for me. I've finally seen the light about the importance of the lead, *la marca,* that defines the man's role in tango. A woman simply doesn't progress without getting to practice with good leads, doesn't gain the requisite confidence to progress, and whether or not they admit it, everyone on the dance floor knows this. It suddenly hit me when I danced with a highly skilled leader who led me effortlessly in moves I had never done before, steps I couldn't have followed with a less experienced dancer. Remember that scene from "Scent of a Woman" when a blind but skillful Pacino manages to lead an *ingénue* who doesn't even know what tango music is? As hokey as it seemed, it told a certain truth about tango, a truth experienced once again when I was turned over to the next partner whose lead I couldn't follow at all in spite of all my experience. I felt like a beginner again, forced to apologize like a beginner for not being able to follow. A flash of anger threatened but didn't erupt; instead a cogent reminder: learning requires the space and permission to make mistakes, thousands of them. In tango, we shelter one another in an embrace as we expose our imperfections to one another.

I understand something else I didn't before. How did I ever wonder why male egos were so affected by tango, so susceptible to the tango blues? Why my own partner and others often suffer from performance anxiety when they are about to dance with a new person? Or when they know this partner is more experienced than they? It's simply the case that men have more responsibility in tango. Period. Larry expresses it this way: "We're expected to take the responsibility/blame for a poor dance whether the follower is a beginner (we should dance to her level and lead perfectly) or advanced (we have no excuse then)."

So what did I do with this insight? I made a pledge to myself to be more magnanimous with my partners in class. After all, the complement to this insight is another—that once beyond the beginning level, instruction is primarily for the leaders. The follower's role from now on is a matter of good form and style: don't anticipate, stay on your axis and in front of the man's chest with lightness, sensitivity, and beautifully controlled foot style. (The latter a woman can get by working at a bar and a mirror mimicking her favorite women dancers and by dancing with good leaders.) Men, on the other hand, have the responsibility for even more than deciding the patterns to lead and navigating the floor. He must also know which foot his partner is on, he must assess the level of his partner, adapt to any mis-followed steps without placing blame and, oh yes, listen to and use the music. All of this in addition to his primary aim: to keep the follower interested enough to want to dance with him again! Instruction and correction being some of what he needs to get all that, the least I can do, I decided, is to be generously patient and open to helping the leader grasp the instruction, without appearing to be bossy.

On the other hand, I decided something entirely contradictory to what I had just written; that I should try not to help a man too much. How will he ever fully understand how important a clear lead is if his follower dances his intentions, as she guesses them to be, rather than what he actually leads? In other words, leaders are best served in classes and *practicas* if the followers don't try to guess what the leader might have intended, but only dance what was clear. In a learning situation, if we follow a muddy lead, if we respond to it as if it is clear, or try to maintain our balance when he's pulling us off balance, aren't we doing a disservice? I'll be chewing on this contradiction for quite a while, I suspect.

That night at the crowded and friendly milonga, a woman we didn't know, glowing with feverish, sweaty joy, slid off the dance floor and onto a seat next to us—as if she'd just hit a home run—wiping her damp brow with a napkin and grabbing a menu to fan herself. "Whew," she almost whinnied, "my hormones are on overtime! I can't believe it. See that man over there."...she pointed, "he's a guest instructor. Did you see me dance with him?" We hadn't actually but that didn't stop her. "Wow... Wow..." she swooned, "that's what it's all about. Heaven! really, heaven. Whew," she fanned herself furiously, "that dance makes the whole evening worthwhile. I don't care if I never dance again! That dance will hold me for a year."

Frank leaned in to another man's ear, whispering wryly, "How'd you like to make a woman feel like *that*?" A man nearby who had witnessed her effusion flashed an expression which, if translated, might read, "I sure wouldn't want to be the next man who dances with her."

Day three. Honoring my promise of last year to my poor feet, I took the day off. I was not, however, planning to give up tonight's milonga. Still in rest mode, what I was most grateful for tonight was not the dancing so much as the opportunity to ask a few questions of teachers about the growing diversity of tango styles. The more experienced I become the more I notice — and try to follow — styles I have never been taught. I heard tonight about the experimental groups forming around people like Fabian Salas, where the point is to push the envelope of tango *clasico*. This group, for example, is exploring questions such as, when opening up from close embrace, are there movement possibilities that don't necessarily derive from salon tango but can instead be original? When dance floor space opens up, we watch for signs of what our companions and others call *tango nuevo* or "new generation" tango. It's obvious that people dancing this way are mostly twenty-somethings. Instead of classically tight and sharp *ganchos* that we've been taught, theirs are big and high and done within the fluid motion of midturn, or combined with other big leg work like high *sacadas*. Everything is done in extreme style: the change of direction with rapid pivots, the large loose steps, dizzying spiral turns and single axis turns, rarely a pause for stationery footwork or foot play, those adornments seemingly abandoned as those of the past. Fascinated now, we watch strictly as audience members, appreciating while knowing full well we'll never pursue this style together. But I have to admit, I'll never turn down an opportunity to dance with a twenty-something who would flatter me by thinking I can actually follow him.

Day four. Today at lunch time, we are shown additional video footage (since last year) for "Chasing the Ghost," a documentary being made by a dancer (Barbara Durr) eager to capture on film the attitudes of the real *tangueros,* those Argentines who began dancing in Tango's glory days and who are now near the end of their lives. We are transfixed by the images of men and women who would never tolerate an interruption of their dance but for a question as worthy of their opinion as "why do you dance tango?

Tango is as necessary as water.

It's not just a way to dance, it's how to walk in life.

Tango is a culture, a culturally distinct way to live.

The woman interprets the feelings a man sends; it's an exquisite partnership in feeling.

You finally begin to understand the lyrics after the age of 50.

Tango is a way to win over death. We know we have limited time. What we may only have is three minutes of tango in a bubble, the supreme moment of our life.

I want to be reincarnated as a bandoneon!

One of the *tangueros* interviewed on the video is the filmmaker's dance partner, whimsically called "Cacho," who turned up in the flesh as the last instructor of the day. Bald and short, with a belly that hangs over his belt, he is clearly not the media image of a suave tango *maestro*, certainly not a tango poster boy, but what he does with tango is obviously what is currently respected and in demand, judging by the number of highly skilled instructors who are taking this class.

Cacho talks passionately about his philosophy as he demonstrates his unique style. He and his partner lean heavily towards each other, not always chest to chest but sometimes allowing for holding on one's side—the two requirements being that (1) the "two axes make one" and (2) pivots are made on both feet rather than on one as normally taught.

Watching him perform at milongas, we had remarked about how distinctive he looked, trucking forward with alternating *rubato* and staccato steps, often planting his partner solidly in a lean while he does some fancy foot work before shifting her gears and her direction and then "driving" her on. This demo he performs, and urges us to practice, explains his style cogently: he has the women placing hands on man's chest, with the instructions to the leader to walk, pause, lead a pivot on both feet with weight in center, and continue walking in that new direction. But to our astonishment, we notice that no one is doing it correctly. The only reason we can fathom is that pivots are so relentlessly taught to be done on one foot, and mostly by the follower, that leaders can't readily break the very few rules tango imposes, and Cacho's style breaks all the rules. Even by the end of the class only a few of the participants are getting it; we're glad we're watching rather than dancing.

He leaves us, though, with some memorable quips. "What are the most important elements of tango?" His answer: "you, the music, your partner, and the space you have to dance in." While the first three are commonly named by other *maestros,* Cacho's addition of the fourth helps to explain the underlying motivation for his style. The leader's pause, hold, and pivot are entirely determined by the space he sees ahead as open and available... a place to move his dance into, and a pivot with which to lead him and his partner there.

After the ball is over*...* The final milonga with live music is a lot cozier this year because it isn't held at the Crystal Ballroom, where we remember "flying" across the vast sprung floor last year. What we'll remember of tonight is a small venue so dense with dancers that we were allowed only small steps and close embrace style, and also the uniquely exciting performances by some of the *maestros:* Evan, Michelle, and Christy perform a tour de force *menage a trois;* Angel and Rosa fuse tango and salsa at top speed, and Eva and Patricio dance a cabaret style tango that surpasses even the flashy cabaret we've seen on competitive ballroom shows.

But what we also take away from this evening is some serious doubt — both self-doubt and doubt about the way tango is best learned. What were we getting out of this expensive and exhausting experience? we had to ask ourselves. The steps we had semi-learned in group classes could not be done at an event like this, a fairly typical big city milonga, because there isn't space enough. The group classes felt mostly unsatisfying for other reasons as well. Frank had admitted he often couldn't lead the women he met in group classes and wasn't sure why; while I could usually follow the men, it was often because I was helping them rather than being led. Those I genuinely couldn't follow were simply superior dancers and snubbed me when it was time to dance again. We left too many group lessons feeling frustrated and dissatisfied. That doesn't mean we regretted the camps we've attended. Not at all. We wouldn't have gotten this far without camps, especially considering our lack of opportunity, in our rural life, to dance regularly at milongas. But perhaps now, at this stage in our dance life, camps would no longer be as useful any more. If we attend camps in the future, we decided, it would be for the fun of their star-studded milongas, not for group instruction.

So, this may be our last tango camp. We decide, at least tentatively, that we may gain more for our tango dollar from taking private lessons from dancers we admire, and by dancing more often, with a variety of dancers, at milongas we can manage to get to. Camps, we decided, have given us the instruction we've needed to get to this point, where we're savvy enough about what we need to make our own new plan.

Only one tinge of regret pressed my imagination as we lifted off from Portland's crowded airport. It happened when Larry described what he'd seen at one of the all-night milongas we were all too tired to attempt. Held at the rambling home-studio of a Portland-based instructor and complete with Arabian Nights tent-draperies, dry ice mist plumes, and crepes for breakfast, it celebrated tango with blatant excess. Dancing with each other mainly, but also open to an invitation from a brave novice, the best dancers no doubt demonstrated the *"tanguedad"* of the elite. My regret lay in the sure knowledge that I'd never be part of the inner guest circle to such a party except in a camp setting like this, that is, through an open invitation to tango campers to enter a rarefied space. Undeniably, it's one of the unheralded and understated benefits of camp attendance, the chance to mix with tango nobility.

This may be the place to mention the special qualities of still another setting for studying tango, one often overlooked: the tango vacation, held usually at a resort or on a cruise ship. If you like the intimacy of smaller groups, which provide a better chance for friendlier contact, and can see yourself combining dancing with vacation mode, the tango vacation is worth considering. In those we have attended, we found that being with people who shared our tango enthusiasm, while relaxing in a beautiful setting, actually raised our attention level for the instruction given. Some of this must have to do with stress reduction and the absence of "busy noise." But just as importantly, lessons limited to a maximum of three hours a day seem more on a human scale, that is, matching our capacity for taking on new information as well as saving our feet for dancing later that evening, if we chose to. Moreover, it's a treat having lessons with excellent teachers who are also on vacation and therefore more relaxed and personal. I'll carry forever my memories of sharing a Mexican breakfast with Cecilia Gonzales and Eduardo Saucedo, talking tango while planning a day hike!

Solos

The single woman who busies herself at the back of a chair, repeating *ochos*. Youngish, saucy and funky in her tiny dress and the highest heels she can tolerate. "This is what the teachers say you should do when you aren't dancing, practice *ochos*." She is making good use of her time. Glancing over her shoulder, shyly, taking in the lucky couples sliding by, she betrays a flash of feeling — she's just as good, why isn't she dancing? She is a regular, she knows the crowd, volunteering her time to sell tickets at the door, but once the tickets are mostly taken, she's primed to move. One inner ankle brushes the other as she practices "collecting" between forward steps, then backward steps. In the last hour, now that men have arrived who know her from classes, or other people's husbands have tired of their usual partners, we have seen her on the floor, showing us her skill, eyes closed, so as to totally concentrate on following. We wonder how without a usual partner at home she can get to be so good. We guess she goes to work, then to tango events and not much else. In the San Francisco Bay Area, it is possible to live that way. She leaves alone. We wonder if she dates any of her partners and how they negotiate a date at a milonga.

Another single woman is the large and lovely one sitting on one of the chairs lining the wall. She smiles brightly at first, her smile fading slowly as the music wears on without her being asked. I watch for her at several times during the evening — she IS dancing finally, and I cheer silently for her even though most of her partners are shorter and slimmer than she. She appears not to notice or if she does, not to care. Neither do they, apparently. The important thing is that she's dancing and they are enjoying her as a partner. She reappears the following year at the same weekend, doing the same thing in a different dress.

I admire these women, enormously. Undaunted by convention, by principles that rule most women, including the need for a man securely at our side in settings dominated by couples, these women relentlessly pursue their love of tango in a solo mode. Maybe what they pursue is that elusive moment between man and woman that is a purely coordinated call and response, syncopated pleasure made to the music of two bodies in harmony even though doing different things. One body, four legs. Better than sex? Certainly less binding, less responsible. A woman can have a sweet hit of sex in vertical position without caring if she gets a phone call the next day. And even if she can't control the number of times she gets to dance, she has choices about where and when she'll dance, when to go home and with whom, if anyone.

It may surprise you, though, to find that some of these solo women are not single. They may have husbands or lovers at home who are non-dancers, but that doesn't stop them from following the tango trail. For some of them, tango is simply a playful, fantasy-life, offering the delight of a mini-affair without the entanglements of being sexual. Most women in this category insist there are no problems ahead for them in having tango as a "hobby." We discuss this topic further in Chapter Four, *The Rewards*.

The solo man is often the more common sight at a milonga, an observation which surprises people who are used to ballroom dances where the opposite is true. These men are swift eyed, eager to practice, or to prove their prowess. They tend to be men who easily become sure of themselves, with good self esteem, some even prone to overestimating their skill. We notice the more fearless among them asking far more skilled women to dance—including other men's wives—and not being refused. Experienced women encourage these men because, like me, they know this is the way these men will improve their lead, and everyone will benefit in the long run. If you go to milongas regularly you might see these same men reappear… and grow more accomplished. The more accomplished they become, of course, the more they are sought out as partners. One such man taking an advanced class with us, a man you would never look at twice on the street—stringy haired, thickly bespectacled, with pencil protector overspilling its contents—danced so elegantly and rhythmically that several women refused to give him up at partner-changing time. I overheard one say, "please save a dance for me tonight." His reply, "well, if you can catch me... I'm pretty much booked up."

I envy the solos on one point: they get to dance with a greater variety of people, a better way to hone one's leading and following skills than dancing primarily with one person. When I admit this though to solos, they balk... "but you have a partner at home to practice with, how lucky you are, how can you complain?"

Overall, I'd say the solo woman is subject to experiencing the best and worst of tango culture. On one occasion she might get to dance every *tanda* with a different man; on another, she might sit on the sidelines most of the evening, having to content herself with small talk with other women. Of course, in our image-conscious society, the younger and slimmer women seem to have an advantage. Even if they are only beginning dancers, they tend to be invited to dance while more accomplished, but older, women may be overlooked. But every woman, no matter what age or size, at one time or another will sit on the sidelines and ask herself, "what does it take to get asked?" "What do I have to do, or be, to dance as often as I'd like to?" American feministas could have a field day with the inequities of the tango world if they chose to take it on. The fact remains that here in North America with traditions of equality and equal opportunity, women do have the option of reversing the Argentine tradition by asking men to dance (allowing them the option to refuse) and by doing so often enough, getting them used to the idea that this is appropriate behavior in a modern society.

That being said, the solo woman who loves tango enough to submit herself to the vicissitudes of tango life, as does the woman in the following story, may find rewards and tribulations inextricably blended.

"By The Wall"

a story

"SOME NIGHTS ARE this way," Charlene thought as her eyes
roamed the large expanse of hardwood and heels. One has to put
up with them once in a while. Dancers drifted past and the floor
looked crowded, but it was far from full. It was one of those nights
when there are a lot more women than men. She could have stayed
closer to home and gone ballroom dancing, but the ballroom dances
seemed flat, now that she'd discovered tango. Or she could have
gone to the regular tango milonga closer to home, but she had ruled
that out, as a trial, to put distance between herself and a married
man. If she were twenty years younger, the ratio wouldn't matter
so much since younger women get asked much more often. Then
again, take off twenty years and she'd still be a lot older than the one
passing her right now, wearing a tight and tiny black dress.

There were worse places to be than sitting on the edge of the
dance floor and watching the tango. It was still better than being at
home alone; she got plenty of that. She could have called a girlfriend
to take in a movie, but most of the best evenings of her life recently
had been on the dance floor. You can never tell how an evening
might develop; the floor demographics could still shift. It doesn't
take a lot of dances to make the effort worthwhile.

Another svelte *tanguera* drifted by with a man holding her close.
Sitting up a little straighter she thought, how could you blame the
men, really, delighting in the accompaniment of all these stunning
younger women? She certainly didn't resent this girl having her time
on the floor. Charlene had taken several classes with her and they
had even had a lunch together; Charlene found her considerate and
charming. The younger woman's partner, though certainly over forty,

might even be closer to her age than to Charlene's. A few more men was all that was needed, men over fifty. Where were they? Watching basketball from the plump safety of their armchair? Reading news magazines in their basement? Darrel came to mind. He'd left her after nineteen years of marriage to be with a woman sixteen years younger and start another family. Charlene knew where Darrel was—crawling around the house exhausted after another forty-five hour work week, chauffeuring a nine and six-year-old to every imaginable socially enhancing activity while his younger wife asks for more. Served him right.

Couples, of course, were abundant, arriving together with rings on fingers and complementary colors. Not that most of them didn't dance with others, but they seemed tonight to be switching with other couples. Charlene had known what it was like to arrive at a dance on the arm of a partner. Herbert was the first one, a traffic engineer with the city. He took ballroom classes three days a week and always attended the Friday night social. Insisting on picking her up even for classes, he would arrive five minutes before he said, wearing the striped shirts for classes and the solids with a tie for the socials. He loved the foxtrot and cha cha, sought out the teacher for the waltz—said it was his best dance—and always made sure that Charlene never danced with two different partners in a row. She never asked him about this, but was sure that it was intentional. If no one asked her to dance, Herbert might dance two or three with friends he knew from classes, but if Charlene danced with someone else, she could count on Herbert being there to grab her for the next one. Sex was for after the socials. He was always there for her, as devoted as a watch dog, until she said that she didn't want to see him romantically anymore, even though, as she said the words, there was an inescapable irony to them. He looked hurt, but was driving another woman to classes the next week. He never asked her to dance again.

Since Darrel, Frank had been her longest relationship. A contractor with three grown kids, they had been introduced at a retirement party for a mutual friend at the university where Charlene worked in Registration. He worked long weeks as a foreman for a large commercial construction operation with offices all over California. He made their time together count, making her feel wanted sexually for the first time since Darrel's affair with their neighbor. Frank reluctantly took dance classes with her, even though it meant returning to the beginning level for Charlene. He had the coordination to be good at it, but one class a week and two dances a month was all she could wring out of him. She occasionally accepted invitations to dance while out with Frank, but he rarely would ask anyone else, said he had to be better first. So Charlene would usually sit with him and wait until he was ready to dance again. After being together for eight months, he was transferred to Sacramento to build a hospital. They saw each other on weekends for two more months, until he apologetically said that they were just too different. She knew that meant that he had found someone who was less different. Aren't differences part of the spark that makes a relationship work, she had asked? *Vive la différence.* French sayings don't always apply in America, was her conclusion.

Charlene had decided long ago that even to have only two or three dances an hour is satisfying. She had arrived just past nine and now it was almost ten and she was yet to dance. The unpadded chair was getting harder and harder. She got up and walked slowly around the room, stopping near a highly visible wall. The wall was about twenty feet wide and stood between the entrance door and the drink bar. It was an off-white blank canvas, except for the row of photos of famous dance teachers that had made guest appearances at the studio. She knew she had a better success rate standing where she could be noticed, rather than sitting. How unbearable though to stand for so long and not be asked. The three inch heels made her feel even more conspicuous. She hadn't worn heels like these since her twenties and never would have again, but in tango a woman dances mainly on the balls of her feet. Also, at five-foot-two, the extra three inches were usually welcomed, however sore her feet and lower back might be the next day. Tall female friends had told her that at least she never had the embarrassment of dancing with a man so short he couldn't see over her to steer through traffic. The one consolation in not dancing all night was that her feet wouldn't hurt.

Two men were talking only twenty feet away; maybe they would notice her. She thought of her coworkers and friends who seemed so impressed by how she had stepped boldly into the world of dance eight years ago by herself, only a year after her marriage ended. When she spoke of the better moments of dance success they would applaud her courage and resolve as if she had floated the Nile in a canoe with only a knife for survival. What would they think of her now, standing alone by the wall and waiting? They should know that this was where the real courage was. She could introduce herself to one of the other single women, but being with another woman in conversation would decrease both of their chances of getting asked. No, this was the price that sometimes had to be paid.

Charlene wondered about her local milonga, who was dancing with whom right now? Best not to dwell on that. Wasn't that why she was here? Who was dancing with Clifton was the question that always mattered. It had happened gradually over two years, building steadily since their first dance, and yet she still didn't really know what was in his mind. Obviously he enjoyed her and would ask for at least one dance every evening. And that was the highlight of every evening. He was sixty-two with over fifteen years of tango experience. Although he still wasn't the most talented of the men, no one's arms felt like his. Just the way that he took her right hand and brought it next to his left shoulder set her in the mood for romance. Without ever hesitating anymore, she nuzzled into his chest and felt like he interpreted the music with her body, like she was the instrument being stroked. If he danced with her early, she wouldn't care if she danced with anyone for several dances afterwards. Later in the evening, if she wasn't on the floor, maybe he would ask again. She so much preferred his touch that she would avoid eye contact with others in hopes of as many dances as possible with Clifton. Charlene would make sure that she sat near him, at the same table if possible. She had become better friends with his wife than she might have normally, just to be closer.

The only one she had ever told these things to was her therapist. Ms. Simpkins had warned Charlene that this obsession with a married man might not be healthy. At the very least, it might make her unavailable for other men. However, ten minutes with Clifton twice a week did more to satisfy her than most sexual relationships she had known. Nevertheless, here she was, on recommendation by Ms. Simpkins, standing alone by the dance floor of another community. Was her therapist right? Was no one asking her to dance because she was emotionally unavailable or were other factors at work?

A man in his fifties thanked his current partner and Charlene sought to catch his eye as he turned. There was a brief recognition, but he headed straight for his glass of water and then to a new partner nearby just returning from the floor herself. They appeared to be friends. How great it must be to be a man at a dance with extra women. She remembered fondly the handful of times in her eight years of experience where there had been more men than women. Every dance she had a partner. She watched women turning men down knowing that a better one would come along soon, though Charlene could never bring herself to refuse any courteous man. Tonight, some of the most discerning of women were lowering their standards. Or going home.

Several faces were familiar from the many milongas that she had attended, but no one she knew well. Finally a couple came in that she recognized from recent classes—Penny and Jeffrey she could count as friends. Frequently, she only got acquainted with the men in classes, since that's who she danced with, but Penny had introduced herself and expressed an affinity for Charlene. They were relatively new to tango, only about a year's experience, which isn't much for this subtly constructed dance. They were hovering around forty years of age and exceedingly polite. Soon after arriving, they took the floor for a set—Penny looking pleased and Jeffrey reflecting awkwardness. Penny gave Charlene a smile of acknowledgement once while passing by the wall where she stood. Soon after they sat down, Charlene surmised that Penny was talking about her to Jeff, who looked her way quickly. When he came over to ask Charlene to dance, she was sure that it was Penny who had encouraged the action. She appreciated the friendly gesture to share one's partner.

Jeffrey took short cautious steps, ambiguous in their temerity, apologizing for mistakes, even when they weren't his, and keeping his partner at least a few inches away. Mainly though, Charlene was relieved to be dancing. He was familiar and good spirited and was turning the corner from beginning *tanguero* to beyond, where he was actually starting to enjoy himself most of the time. He wore clothes that befit an office job, slacks and a solid green button up shirt. A dance with Jeffrey wasn't enough to make the drive from the North Bay to the Peninsula worthwhile, but at least she was on the floor. The song ended and his arms released her on cue.

"You get better every month, Jeff."

"It's only because you're such a talented dancer that we looked good at all."

With a hand on her back, he had started moving them in the direction of Penny. A man swooped in before they were halfway there and stole his pretty wife away. "Oh well," Charlene said, "she'll come back. Would you dance with me again in the meantime?"

"Looks like it was meant to be," he returned. A bit fatalistic, she thought. At least he didn't say, "Looks like we're stuck with each other."

He danced a little closer this time and wasn't so tentative. Something was missing still. Passion? Did he bring passion to the dance with Penny? Clifton would find every pause that a song contained and squeeze and twist her gently as if her own chest was the bandoneon that was emitting its accordion-like tones. When the violin soared, he would raise his forearm into her back and she would hover as if weightless, hanging on a phrase of notes and determining when and how they would move again.

At the end of the second dance, Jeffrey led her back to their table. Penny was still being led around the floor and would be for two more dances. Charlene thought of asking Jeff to dance again, but she had initiated the second dance and he must know that she would gladly say yes. Maybe he thought he needed to stand watch so that Penny wouldn't be whisked away again. The man dancing with her was certainly holding her tight and Penny looked comfortable. So Jeff and Charlene watched the dancers with only an occasional casual phrase. She considered thanking Jeff and taking leave in order to dance again when Penny broke the hold and ended the embrace with her partner. A balding and fleshy man in his fifties, he politely walked her back to her seat.

"Irv, this is my husband, Jeffrey and my friend, Charlene. Charlene's a very good dancer." Bless her heart. A man would get branded insensitive if he were to walk away from such an introduction. Now Charlene could thank her friend for two partners, even if it was just a convenient way to send him on.

Irv was astute on protocol. "If she's even half as good as you, I'd be delighted."

"She's better than I am, for sure."

Irv took her out on the floor and she soon could tell that he was experienced and easy to dance with. He knew a lot of steps, too and was intent on flashing them before her, like a resume. Charlene was proud of her ability to keep up. Finally, she was in the midst of the dance.

But it didn't last. Abruptly, at the end of the first song, Irv said, "Your friend is right, Charlene, you dance very well. Thank you. I promised someone a dance and I want to catch her before she goes. So maybe later?" Or maybe not. Maybe if all the pretty girls are taken... Charlene walked back to the wall and stood straight and available. All the men were dancing or talking. If they wanted to socialize, why did they come to the dance? She stood alone for three dances and then took a seat on the edge of the dance floor away from anyone who could lessen her chances.

Dancing again had reminded her how much she enjoyed it, even with partners like Jeffrey and Irv, who, although courteous, didn't appear to delight in her company. Couples slinked by, prowling and caressing with the same partner for fifteen to twenty minutes and then switching with others already dancing. Two women who came together, perhaps five years older and another twenty pounds heavier than herself, left without ever dancing. The room was starting to look bigger, the large dark aluminum-rimmed picture windows looming like missing teeth in a monstrous mouth. Charlene preferred crowds that spilled out of their space, crowds that hugged you with their sheer mass. This room was beginning to resemble a solar system with distant planets in orbit around a light that was too far away to feel the warmth.

She didn't like the mood she was dropping into, self-doubting with a splash of resentment like graffiti on a well painted wall. Envy was another word that poked through the well-tended lawn of her mind like a deep-rooted weed. In ten years, she thought, she would look back on her fifty-six year old body of today with longing. Why not revel in today's body right now? This rallied her spirit and brought back a more familiar optimism. But she still wasn't dancing. Even just being asked to dance was a pleasure in itself. She was weary of the convention of men being the ones who had to initiate. She was bolder than most women and would ask friends to dance regularly. Here though, she hardly knew anyone beyond the recollection of faces from other dances. What would go through a man's mind if I asked him to dance, she wondered? Would I look desperate? Inappropriately forward? A man ought to feel complimented by being asked. Most women she had talked to about this tradition thought it fine for a woman to ask a man to dance, they just never did it themselves. She couldn't find anything wrong with it. This wasn't Argentina, after all.

Charlene watched for a while more. It was eleven-thirty and the dance wouldn't go on that much longer. Already a few couples had left. One couple parted on the floor and the man walked in Charlene's direction. She had noticed him several times this evening and remembered him, on occasion, at the larger milongas up north. He was swarthy, perhaps Latino, wearing a gray suit with thin black stripes. His dancing was polished enough to be that of a teacher. The voice inside her said no, the voice that seems to only know one word and repeats it on cue anytime she considers doing anything that involves a risk, but she willed herself out of the chair and towards him. He saw her approach, stopped to let her pass, and looked startled at the question addressed in his direction.

"Would you dance with me?" she asked.

She knew that if he said no, she'd have to get her coat and leave.

"Let me just say something to the couple by the door before they leave and I'll be happy to."

He indeed caught a couple at the door and engaged them. Charlene had to retreat from the floor out of the way of dancers. Where to stand? Best to make it easy to be found. She followed him and stood at the point on the dance floor nearest the door, by the familiar wall adorned with the triumphant personalities that had once graced this floor, and turned to face the dancers. As she did her eye caught the last picture on the wall; it was of the man she had just asked to dance. Her heart raced. Well that was bold of you, Charlene! What a silly thing to get so worked up about, she admonished herself. Why shouldn't I get to dance with the best? Maybe as a teacher, he's even more used to it. He wouldn't forget. The first song finished and another began. She glanced quickly and saw that they were still talking. There weren't that many songs left.

"Would you like to dance?" came from a voice at her side. Like a glass from the table next to you that falls and breaks on the floor, she snapped her head around and saw gray hair and dark bushy eyebrows. Under them was an inquisitive face and beckoning smile. Damn, this was new territory.

"Umm…" she glanced back around at her partner in waiting, "the man by the door is going to dance with me after he finishes his conversation. I would love to have the dance after that, though, if you're still available."

"If I am, I'd be glad to. Enjoy your dance with Victor, he's one of the best."

Her only unsolicited offer moved slowly off around the room. She felt an immediate misgiving, an angst not unlike the atmosphere of a tango song. Another woman had joined the three talking by the door, a woman that Victor had danced with many times that evening.

Meanwhile, the great indiscriminate inner voice was elaborating on its usual contradicting themes. "You can't dance with Mr. Eyebrows until after Victor. Victor only said he'd be right back to be nice. You shouldn't bother Victor, he's busy. That's probably his wife, you know. I told you not to ask, now look what happened. This is only a dance, don't get so worked up — you won't be able to dance well now anyway." She kicked the little voice in the shins and briskly closed the thirty feet to the head of gray hair. Before she could tap him on the shoulder he had engaged another woman in conversation. Damn! Charlene wanted to disappear. She knew enough not to make eye contact with those around her; her inner voice was bad enough, she didn't want to see puzzled and pitying expressions. This would have been another place where crowds were useful. She couldn't just about-face and walk back. Maybe when Mr. Eyebrows took his current partner out on the floor she could discreetly creep back by the door.

She wondered what Ms. Simpkins would have to say about this night? Charlene took a couple of steps off the dance floor. Another song ended and a new one began; another song of passion and caring that was the tango. Victor was still talking. Was he avoiding her after all? Then she noticed that Eyebrow's friend had put her coat on and was carrying her dance shoes. He was just saying goodbye! Charlene let the woman pass and hurried over.

"Excuse me, maybe I'll catch Victor later instead. Is the offer still open?"

"Absolutely." He smiled and led her to the dance floor.

Charlene's new partner held her securely and was listening to the same beat she was. Soon he would have a name. Her body released to the rhythm of another and the satisfying caresses on a dance floor by someone with which you shared the same desire, however transient.

"Last dance," was announced. As they passed the all too familiar wall of photos, she saw that everyone was dancing except for the presenters of the event who were in a discussion by the front desk. Victor had also joined the floor with the woman who had been standing by him. Had he first checked to see if Charlene was still waiting? Charlene settled into the richness of the current dance, the compelling downbeat and sensual phrases of melody. For a moment, she was again a part of the dance.

The Human Factor—Intimacy Required

How intimate are you willing to be on a dance floor with strangers, or, for that matter, your spouse? While it is possible to dance in an open style rather than the chest to chest of close embrace, even the basic movements resemble a caress or a request to engage in a meaningful dialogue. You've got to be ready to care for your partner—even love him—for that short period of time.

To dance tango well—maybe you've guessed, or already know by now—means making yourself vulnerable, vulnerable to the music and vulnerable to your partner, whether leading or following. Making oneself vulnerable means taking emotional risks and allowing exposure to intimacy—at least for three minutes at a time, the usual length of one song. How one handles the tango experience of vulnerability, though, can dramatically influence that dancer's personal life.

Most couples who take up tango together report a positive effect on their relationship, tango adding a welcome spark, acting almost like a new aphrodisiac. For these couples, changing partners and recreating (or simulating) intimacy with others poses no lasting threat. Other couples, though, might go through a bit of trauma along with their lessons, in the form of jealousy or intimidation. Watching your mate dance better with another partner can be painful, for the beginner especially. Fearing that your mate will get carried away by a perceived competitor who is holding him/her closely and happens to be better looking, more skilled, and more worldly than you, can be a humbling experience for anyone. We offer no remedy, only a warning. (The story "Not An Easy Dance," page 122 speaks to this theme.) Three minutes of a shared musical intimacy can be just that, nothing more, and for most people, it is a fully satisfying pleasure. On the other hand, a tango floor may be where you find your soul-mate; hopefully it won't be where you lose the wonderful one you already have.

Another common threat posed by tango's call for vulnerability is the potential toll on one's self-esteem. You may remember that we stressed the need for self-confidence in order to make progress in tango. To maintain one's self-esteem through the process, men especially are reminded to leave off expecting too much of themselves in the early stages, even throughout the first few years of tango practice. It is all too easy to watch the pros and then feel totally inadequate, forgetting that the pros (and the truly dedicated amateurs) have probably been dancing five nights a week for many years.

That admission, though, doesn't help some couples get over the bump that tango can make in their relationship. A man who doesn't make as much progress as his wife/partner or who is less motivated to "get it" to her satisfaction, is likely to lose confidence and then detour from the tango trail. The pressure that this discrepancy in desire can put on their relationship is undeniable. We've seen several couples go through this conflict, calling tango "a harsh mistress"; not that they separated over it, but they dropped tango and one of the partners grieved deeply for the loss, leading to sadness all around. Sometimes, rarely, one of the partners feels free enough to seek tango apart from the other and still be able to maintain their original close relationship.

Even though the common wisdom among dancers is that the woman determines how closely a couple will dance, by the way she steps into her partner's arms and toward his chest, I have found that just as often the degree of close encounter, or level of intimacy, can be determined by the leader. He after all, by convention, takes his partner's right hand in his and then reaches around her back. How far he reaches gives her body a message about how close their encounter will be, in most cases, throughout the dance, with the exception being the current American habit of opening up or closing the embrace to move between two styles, usually in response to rhythm and tempo. Some leaders always dance in close embrace out of choice, their growing sense of personal style requiring they be consistent, well practiced, confident in that choice.

The major challenge for the follower, speaking as a follower now, is to relax enough in the arms of a stranger to forget all the things that might throw you—your self-consciousness about intimacy, your fear of making mistakes and being humiliated, your fear of revealing your inadequacies—and simply relax enough to follow. Don't apologize if you misstep. Don't speak at all, in fact. Be open to the ardor and the longing implicit in the music and give yourself up to it, for at least the few minutes you are in this person's arms. Savigliano calls it "making intimate confessions in public." (Savigliano: 212)

Even Susana Miller admits to the emotional conflicts tango intimacy is capable of arousing: "There were things that were very revealing for me" she said in an interview… "in regard to the capacity to give myself. I used to think my surrender was much more absolute than what it really was. And I faced the fact that I was as afraid of the other sex as the rest of the world. And nobody knows how fearful is the opposite sex…I realized that if I cannot surrender in tango, I cannot dance. To dance I have to surrender."

It's asking a lot of a follower. And that's not all of course that is asked of followers… and leaders too, for that matter. There are those who chase tango and never catch it. For some, it may be simply that they don't want it enough. For others it may be that they expect too much of tango. Tango will not satisfy all of one's emotional needs. Nor is it a substitute for sex. But the way it brings all these needs to the surface and meddles with them can lead us on a fascinating journey to somewhere we've never been.

Of course the journey may be different for each member of a couple. As you'll see in the following story, if there is a disparity in their levels of need, self-confidence, and trust in each other, the tango experience can become an obstacle to a couple's mutual bliss. After all, there's a good deal of ego being messed-with when one's mate is in someone else's arms. In the story following this one, the situation is quite different although also driven by ego-protection. Two strangers, sexually drawn to each other and well-matched on the dance floor, jeopardize a possible future by concealing the truth about their pasts.

"Not an Easy Dance"

a story

"Is something wrong, Eric?"

He didn't answer right away. Eric steered their red Miata away from the curb. Leoma was about to speak again when Eric responded, "What makes you think something's wrong?"

"Because I'm happy and you're not. Is it about something that happened on the dance floor or are you still bothered from when I criticized the shirt you wore tonight?"

They waited at a light in silence, no cars passing from the perpendicular street. "I don't know how to say this without sounding like a prude," Eric said.

"You think I'm dancing with too many men?"

The light changed and Eric worked through the gears. "No…Yes. It's not that simple."

"I didn't mean…"

"It bothers me to see you pressed up against all these different men. I know what they're feeling and fantasizing because I know what it feels like to have your breasts rubbing against my chest and my hand on your naked back."

Leoma checked her seatbelt and pulled it a little tighter. "We've always danced with others. Have you always been bothered and not said?"

"Argentine tango is different." Eric turned onto the Highway 80 on-ramp heading towards the Bay Bridge.

"Because of the close dance position? You get to hold other women the same way. Should I be upset at them putting their breasts against you and thinking licentious thoughts?"

Traffic was fast, but dense, even for a Saturday midnight. Cars were changing lanes quickly and often with little room between vehicles.

Eric started to speak a couple of times and stopped. In the third try came, "Maybe you should be."

"What's that suppose to mean? Is there something going on I should know about?"

"No, I'm sorry. I didn't mean that like it sounded." Eric backed off of a car that changed lanes immediately in front of them. "What I meant was, shouldn't couples that really care about each other feel at least uncomfortable seeing their lover in the arms of another?"

"Only if they're afraid of losing them." Leoma put her hand on Eric's leg. "I like knowing that other women find you attractive. I don't think you're going to leave me because some leggy blond dances a tango with you." They passed through Treasure Island with its history of military base occupation; what prime real estate it could be, though the traffic access would be horrific. "Do you think I'm seriously considering my dance partners as options to run off with?"

"No, I don't think that's what's going through your mind. I don't know. I shouldn't have brought it up."

"If it bothers you, it's important that we talk about it." The exceedingly long and straight bridge with its five lanes on top and five underneath spilled out onto a confusion of intersecting highways. "You didn't dance much without me this evening. Why don't you ask more women to dance?"

Traffic lightened as they turned north on the other side of the bridge. "Because I was one of the worst dancers there. It's embarrassing when women dance just one song with me to be nice and then run away before I can ask for a second. You're taking twice as many classes as me and it shows."

"Women love to dance with you!"

"You don't see their expressions. The couples we see at every dance make it look so effortless, but I try as hard as I can and still don't get it. It might require more time than I'm willing to give it." Eric started to change lanes to the right just as a truck one lane over to his right started to move left. He swerved the Miata back into their lane. "Whoa! I don't think he ever saw us."

"It's a good thing you're alert. You might have just saved my life!"

Leoma looked over with a big flirtatious smile which he never saw, his eyes on the traffic.

Eric pulled in behind the truck and made his way over to the Gilman exit. The Miata coasted into the off ramp and soon they were onto city streets. "Our life seemed smoother when we danced salsa twice a month and you had your aerobics dance on the same nights I went to the gym."

"But that wasn't being together," Leoma said softly.

Eric saw that he was gaining on a police car and slowed down. "We were apart in some ways, but I felt like there wasn't anything separating us."

"Tango doesn't take me away from you, it just makes us stretch."

"Why should we have to stretch to be a couple?"

They pulled off the main street to their neighborhood of small bungalows, where nobody else was returning at one in the morning from tango. The trucks still rumbled on San Pablo. Rap music from a closer car, cycling in an even lower frequency than the trucks, traveled through the street and up their legs, never getting higher than the stomach. It was a quiet neighborhood for the city. The Miata in the driveway, Eric rifled through keys for both door locks to allow him and his wife to enter their rented space.

The aquarium hummed. The message light flashed with a careless rhythm. Leoma took off her coat and slid her hands over her breasts while Eric hung his coat in the closet. He turned around and there she was. She put her arms around his neck and leaned her vulnerable midriff against him while she strained on her tiptoes. His hands surrounded her waist, then moved to the coolness of her back, where she hid nothing. The heater came on, followed by the refrigerator—a harmony of maintenance, so much energy.

"Isn't this all that matters? That my breasts are pushed against only you at the end of the evening?"

"Then why do we do all the other stuff?"

"Because there's music to dance to we might never find any other way. And it's music that goes straight to my heart."

Eric did indeed feel her heart, spread open against his, a heart with a vast wilderness he had never ventured to explore, a terrain so wild it is incapable of dispatching an articulated invitation, but needs to be entered willfully, and once inside, navigated without a map, for there isn't one.

Leoma stretched and leaned into Eric until their chests expanded and contracted in opposite union, his hands already finding their way through buttons. "You know you're the only man whose hands get to wander where they please," she said. In this, she was content. There was no reason to tell Eric that his embrace on the dance floor tonight was not her favorite.

"In a Half Light"

a story

ARTURO VELASQUEZ WRAPPED his arm around his new partner and caught the unmistakable scent of Coco Channel perfume; he had always loved details, which served him well as a radio car policeman and then a brief stint as a detective in his native Los Angeles. That was before the violence and depressive nature of nearly every assignment wore him down to retirement after eleven years. She was about his height and half of his girth, allowing him to encircle her with ease. She rested her face ever so softly against his and waited to be moved. When the music began, he twisted her gently to feel her balance, and, just to feel her. The song was a modern piece with a lot of dynamic variation and, more importantly, long pauses. Perfect, he thought.

Olga Korviskaya appreciated well groomed men who wore a tie and coat to even the weekly milongas; perhaps it was a connection to the old world or her last memory of her father before her mother had escaped with her from the Soviet Union when she was only seven. She had spent much time in the company of men in her twenty adult years, most of it involving their financial generosity for her natural gifts. Lately, she had made a career change and had explored meeting men under much different circumstances. It had been a supreme delight to discover tango, where she could be seductively close to men and rarely have to deal with further entreaties when the song was over. The man that drew her to his chest now was terribly strong, she could tell even through the sport coat, but had gentle hands. She felt safe—a feeling woefully lacking in her earlier profession. From his looks and talent, he might also be an Argentinean.

Arturo placed her carefully on one foot and then another to the strongly punctuated beat of the music. During the frequent pauses and stretched measures he would hold her tighter and lean her against his chest. She acquiesced without a flinch, as most partners did, allowing a delicate and mutual intimacy with a woman. As far as he was concerned, it was the greatest thing the world had to offer.

Arturo had come a long ways from the kid who lived for the fight in San Fernando, a suburb of Los Angeles. Oddly, his first distaste for violence happened while boxing in the Marines and he gave his opponent a concussion. He hardly knew the guy; he wasn't even a compadre, just an Anglo guy from a different base. Somehow, when he found out that the boxer had a kid, he cared about his well being and was greatly relieved when the guy recovered. Soon after that he retired from boxing; it requires hurting your opponent or being hurt and neither appealed to him anymore. His first few years on the police force were a good fit. He enjoyed the variety and challenge. Life on the street had been his early education. Even the violence seemed for a purpose and was only used when necessary. It was once again a child, this time his own, that birthed a change of heart in him. He witnessed too many murders, over half of them young and too many looks of hate directed his way, especially by his own people. One day he picked up his ten-year-old son from school, he and his wife already divorced, and discovered the boy had been in a fight. At that moment, he didn't even know what the fight was about, but his capacity for the face of violence had been saturated. He knew he couldn't do what he was doing anymore.

The tempo increased and their steps became shorter. Olga responded, grateful to have these moments where she didn't have to think and plan. Throughout the waking day her mind wove through the labyrinth of calculation and concern; now she could close her eyes and be carried along. Not that suspending her willful resolve was easy for even these few minutes at a time. It had taken well over a year to be comfortable and graceful with most leaders on the dance floor. She had always been attracted to dance, but felt the need to avoid most large social venues while working in the strip clubs and even for the escort service in Santa Monica. Once in a discotheque with a girlfriend who didn't know of her true occupation, two men had recognized her from the club she worked at and passed word around the bar. At first her friend was intrigued by the sudden interest guys were giving the two of them, but became horrified when the propositions started and they asked her if she was also a stripper. Their friendship never recovered.

When she first dared to explore partner dancing, she avoided West LA where a large portion of her clients lived and drove the hour into the Valley. Then, after nearly a year of anonymity, a man she had escorted only once several years before saw her and asked her to dance before she could make an exit. He was polite and discreet, but he began offering her increasing amounts of cash to spend the night with him and she suddenly felt exposed and vulnerable. Her beloved life of tango and ballroom suddenly wasn't safe anymore. Olga's internet clothes business had started paying a living wage, so she left LA for San Francisco within a month. She had to work as a waitress as well to afford living here, but at least she had made the break at the age of thirty-eight, before age forced it on her, from a life she had begun to loathe. Now that she had discovered tango, she would do anything necessary, outside of the sex trade, to live within distance of the exciting Bay Area dance scene.

The music took a sudden leap in pace and volume culminating in a fast piano run and an abrupt close. He led her in a rapid circular pattern, flipping her back again and freezing her against him as the last beat flared. Without the prop and permission of the music, their dramatic pose dissolved swiftly in the ensuing silent interlude. He returned her weight to both feet and extended a compliment, "You dance very well."

"You were easy to follow."

"I haven't seen you dancing around here before, but you're obviously not a beginner. Are you new in town?"

"I just moved here from Chicago."

"Chicago lost a good dancer."

"Thank you. The Bay Area tango scene is so much better."

"Who are some of the teachers in Chicago?" he asked. She hoped to hell he didn't know anyone in Chicago and made up names on the spot with a Spanish surname. "I haven't heard of them,' he responded, "but there are a lot of teachers across the country now that tango's catching on. Is Marie Talisman teaching in Chicago?"

Olga had no idea who this woman was, though she had taken lessons from a few traveling teachers in LA. "There was a Marie who taught across town, but I never took from her and don't remember her last name. That could be the same woman. I think she left though."

"I think we're impeding traffic here," Arturo began as couples bumped and negotiated around them. "Dance with me again?" She accepted and he merged her into the passionate sea of *tangueros*. It was a faster piece with a steady rhythm that encouraged constant progress. The leader still had the option of how to approach the dance; he could attempt difficult maneuvers of flash and brilliance to wow onlookers and, perhaps, impress his partner, or, he could hold her close and dance the *milonguero* style with relatively simple rapid and short steps. He was experienced enough now to carry off either and he figured his partner was too, but the overwhelming draw of the dance was the wonder of this woman in his arms that he had only known for five minutes. Where else could he be so close so fast? Of course, he did know where else. For a few hundred dollars he could choreograph an entire evening of intimate physical contact with a beautiful woman. What was always lacking though was the woman's desire for him; prostitutes guard themselves carefully from opening their hearts to a client. When, fifteen years ago, he first saw his wife's eyes look back at him without the desire, a feeling like a cold wind ripped through his belly and cut him in two. The path from his mind to his sexual being was severed. Now, women wanted to dance with him. Women of all ages and backgrounds wanted the same safe vehicle of intimacy that tango offered. He let his consciousness rest on the warm supple body in his arms, wondering about the person who resided within.

She was relieved to be dancing again, safely beyond the conversation of her fabricated past. He was guiding her through hypnotically simple steps that let her mind relax. Olga had decided soon after leaving LA to construct a vague general history of being a waitress in Chicago. She had studied a map of the Windy City and read a travel book to sound credible, both of which had saved her story a couple of times. At first, the lie was fun, even sexy, but lately it was accompanied by a hollow feeling.

They danced for a total of four songs with only a couple of words between the last numbers. The fourth song marked the end of a set and a time for the floor to reshuffle. "I really enjoyed dancing with you, especially the last tango waltz; seemed like we found a groove. By the way, my name's Art."

"I'm Olga." She offered her hand and he took it in a quick gesture, both of them laughing lightly at the casual protocol, considering their having just been wrapped around each other for fifteen minutes.

"Could I get you a drink?"

"That would be nice of you. Some lemony soda, maybe?" Arturo thought they would walk to the bar together, but she apparently expected him to bring it back so he walked briskly off, not wanting to leave this beauty alone for long. His last glance had captured the image of her tightly contoured high neck, high hemmed dress and the soft mounds underneath.

"Arturo, *ese* — you gonna walk right by me now?" He had almost breezed by Leticia without seeing her. Leticia had been a friend since his first days in the Bay Area. They had a handful of torridly seductive evenings together while they were seeing others, only to break it off very suddenly when her serious lover proposed. She was still with her husband, though he never took to dance. Arturo had no idea where his girlfriend of that time had gone. Somehow, he and Leticia had retained a friendship, greatly aided by the world of dance. Each time they danced they stirred up the smoldering coals buried in the ash, but they never allowed enough fresh air into the mix to catch fire again.

"Letty! *Como va la mas bonita?* How's the hottest dancer in San Francisco been this week?

"*Siempre lista para bailar.* At first I thought you were coming over to dance with me, but now it looks like you've got a new serious interest going on. So tell me about her. Where'd you find her?"

"I just met her here fifteen minutes ago. Her name's Olga and she just moved here from Chicago."

"And she's *guapa* and likes you, no?"

"Beautiful, yes. It's a little early to tell what she thinks of me."

"Of course she does—all the girls want to dance with Arturo. You almost stole me away on my wedding day from a man I love very much, even though he dances like a robot. Even now she's very jealous that you're talking to another woman and ignoring her."

"She's not even looking this way."

"That doesn't mean she isn't watching. You're still a slow learner with women."

"I was on my way to get us drinks. Can I catch you for a dance *mas tarde?*"

"Have I ever turned you down for a dance?" He kissed her cheek and walked quickly off to the refreshment bar. While the guy behind the counter readied their drinks, Arturo glanced back towards Olga and saw that one of the regular *tangueros* had engaged her in conversation, probably asking her to dance. He paid for the drinks, turned around, and saw Olga striding on to the dance floor with the tall man from the East Bay. That's all he remembered about the guy, even though he was probably in the same room with him twice a week at dances. At first, he felt angry; he had only stopped for a minute with Letty. Then he checked himself. "I dance with a woman for fifteen minutes, have a lemon soda in my hand, and expect tango fidelity?" he thought humorously. His next thought was to dance with Leticia, but she had been snatched up instantly, like normal. So, he walked the drinks back to Olga's chair and set them underneath.

Olga had danced with Brian before and enjoyed it. He was talented, polite, and didn't ask questions. Art was still talking very animatedly to a beautiful woman when she accepted Brian's invitation to dance. It would be silly to sit and wait for a man just because he's bringing you a drink. Nevertheless, she had a strong first attraction to Art and didn't want him to wander off thinking she wasn't interested. She saw that Art had brought the drinks back to where she had been sitting. He looked over in her direction and she felt an odd jolt of memory, like she had met him before; he wasn't smiling now and his eyes were asking questions. He didn't stay there for long before asking a woman nearby to dance.

Several dances later, she thanked Brian and walked off towards her chair, hoping that Art would see her. Before Olga even made it to her chair though, she saw that he had gone back to the woman he had talked to by the bar who slid immediately into his arms like she belonged there. Olga watched as Art led his familiar partner through a dazzling array of flashy moves to fast music. She added flair whenever possible with leg lifts and quick flirting caresses of Art. Olga had thought that she had danced well with Art, but now saw that he was used to a lot better. Then came the glance. There wasn't recognition, but his partner had looked to see if Olga was watching and then smiled with satisfaction and kept tight against Art. Olga dropped her eyes to her drink and didn't challenge the alpha female. A man asked her to dance and she accepted, glad to be off the sidelines. He was not an experienced dancer and at times it was sloppy. Still, it was better to be dancing than dwelling on the demise of a short fantasy.

All right then, he wasn't going to wait around either. He had asked the woman closest to him to dance and joined the tight mesh of *tangueros*. He took courteous care of his current partner, but his thoughts were on Olga. Damn, a woman could get under his skin quick. A few songs holding her and some mysterious chemical bond starts to form. Thankfully it didn't happen that way with most of them, but when it did it grabbed and twisted his will. Did he just want to have sex with her, he wondered? There wasn't a woman in the room that he thought sexier than Leticia, but several years on the other side of their sexual affair he could play and flirt with her on the dance floor and not feel that same obsession. Had he just planted his seed and moved on? Was Olga just the next in a long line? How would he ever the hell know if someone was more than this when the unavoidable blinders of lust forever filtered his vision?

At the end of the second song, he glanced at Olga to see if she was still with her partner and couldn't tell whether they were going to dance another or not. Then he saw Leticia separate and made a quick break from his partner and caught Letty before anyone else could. She moved into his arms like a lover and he used the restrained rush of his new desire for someone else to blast them past the gravity of pretense to the freedom of passionate space. With Letty's predilection for exhibiting her talents and Arturo's progressing knowledge of the dance, they had created a reputation for putting on a show. The floor wouldn't clear, but he knew that they would be noticed by everyone. In an odd way, Letty felt like his wife when they danced—so much shared intimacy and well known curves to place his hands. And he never had to be anxious about her desire to be with him in tango or that he would lose her through an evening of dancing with others. Another man was known as her husband, but on the dance floor, he believed she would always be his, more so than to any other.

"Bravo, Arturo! You know that you are still my favorite dance partner, don't you?" He didn't answer because he didn't have to. "Your new love interest is sipping on the drink you bought her. Why don't you introduce me—let her know that I'm just the woman you enjoy dancing with more than anyone else in the world and not a romantic threat."

"We only just met."

"All the better. Don't be such a *burro*." And she led him off towards Olga, careful to walk a half step behind so that she appeared innocent.

Olga looked up timidly, he thought, as they approached. "Olga, I'd like you to meet my long time friend Leticia."

"Call me Letty. Arturo says that you're one of the best dancers he's been with in a long time."

"Pleased to meet you. I may not seem so good after he's danced with you."

"Nonsense. Art and I are just so used to dancing together that we can really let loose. Since my husband barely dances I need someone to appreciate me. Besides, who better to take care of me than Detective Velasquez?"

"You're a detective?"

"Was. I'm Deputy Director of Security now for the Oakland Coliseum."

"But you were a cop and detective for eleven years in Los Angeles. He just got tired of chasing drug dealers and busting prostitutes. Arturo says that you just moved here from Chicago. What do you do?"

"I'm a waitress," she stammered. Not wanting to say too much, but needing to say more, she continued "and working on an internet business."

"What kind of business?"

"An on-line store for clothes." Sexy clothing, many never meant for wearing in public or to be kept on long, but Olga didn't want to share these details.

"Women's clothes? I'd like to see it."

"It's being reconstructed now, but maybe in a week or two." Maybe by then she would have forgotten or it wouldn't matter.

"Well let me know when I can see what you've created. In the meantime, I've kept you away from dancing with Art long enough. It was good to meet you."

Arturo offered his arms and Olga hid her face next to his. Was it him? If he recognized her, he gave no indication. One of the detectives that investigated the overdose at the party three years ago had been Latino. She had been drunk herself and the memory was blurry, but something was horribly familiar. At least she had been wearing a long curly blonde wig that night, at the request of her patron. She closed her eyes and followed as best she could. Stepping backwards blindly is the fate of a woman dancer, she thought. Thank God she hadn't said she was from LA. Maybe she should have moved to Chicago all along. Why had she mentioned the internet business? Damn it! Why couldn't she have a normal on-line business? Because that's what she knew and had the connections, and, it paid so much better. Was that wrong? Did it have to carry the price of disrespect? She knew her mind was racing ahead and began to pull back on the reins. Nothing had happened yet. He probably wasn't even the same detective. "Detective Velasquez," why did she call me that, Arturo thought? Sure, some women are aroused by "lawmen," maybe Letty was even one of them, but most tango women aren't. He guessed from Olga's expression that she wasn't either. Now he would have to be extra sensitive and courteous to avoid images of someone carrying a badge and about to make an arrest. So, he held Olga softly and didn't push the edge of improvisation; better for the dance to be smooth than to risk her feeling judged if she can't keep up. The rhythm had a deliberate pulse and he relished the rocking of her breasts against his chest while they turned. Lyrics jumped from the music to be caught by the few Spanish speakers.

> The half-light where we meet,
> bewitches us with love,
> a half-light shades our kisses,
> a half-light from above.
> My twilight here with you,
> is in a half-light too.
> A smooth and gentle velvet
> is the half-light of our love.

They danced several songs before taking a break. When they walked back to the chairs, talking was awkward. He asked her about Chicago, but she was reticent to say much. She asked him why he was no longer a detective and Arturo stumbled through references about "growing tired of the violence" and all the sad experiences. She rarely met his eyes and he started thinking that making a connection with her beyond the dance floor might be more difficult than it was worth. His friend's statement that "all beautiful women are damaged goods" popped into his head. He had refuted this crass idea when his friend had uttered it. His rebuttal was that everyone was damaged and that he and his friend just never bothered with a woman unless she *was* beautiful. Olga had her story, but he could see that it wasn't for the casual listener. He felt the need for a break.

"I've really enjoyed dancing with you. Save me another dance for later?" She agreed, but he couldn't tell whether she was relieved or felt rejected. Maybe he should let her alone; perhaps he was looking for way too much from a first evening. Perhaps she just wants to dance and, being beautiful, has to fend off constant unwanted attention.

As he walked off and began to scan the room for available dancers, he too felt relieved. Nothing like wanting an inaccessible woman to mess up an otherwise enjoyable evening, he thought.

How quick things could change. His caress in the dance had been so endearing that she would have gladly kept dancing with him all night. Then they took a break and attempted conversation, but she could think of little to say—her past was to stay hidden and her present too shallow. Now he was off dancing with others. That was the convention; dance a few dances with someone and move on, Olga thought. Not all that different than the sex trade in that one respect, though so much more equal and satisfying. Yet, she had begun wanting more in her life than a shuffle of partners limited to only a thin veneer of who she was. A stranger asked her to dance and she accepted. In her mind she fantasized a query, "Hi, I'm Olga, an ex-stripper and prostitute turned cocktail waitress and sexy internet clothing entrepreneur. This won't hurt our chances at a respectful and meaningful relationship, will it? You're a contractor. How nice. Of course that doesn't mean that I'm going to expect free home repairs tonight now does it?"

Her current partner was at least ten years younger than herself, but nevertheless, a talented dancer. With intense focus he kept her moving through a myriad of steps, keeping more distance to allow for more complicated patterns. Tango like this reminded her of other dances—deliciously fun, but less intimate. Maybe she could be honest with most people, she thought. This young man probably wouldn't care or might even find her more intriguing. Tango, after all, was born on the streets and in the brothels of Buenos Aires, wasn't it? At least that was the modern folklore. Yet, it made her feel so vulnerable to think of her past being public. If one person knew, wouldn't it spread through the dance community like any tasty gossip? "I'm dancing with Olga the harlot. No, excuse me, the ex-harlot." How could she flirt and play like a regular woman with this label? Public opinion wasn't kind towards women of her past profession. She had a reoccurring nightmare of trying to find where she had parked her car. Always, it would be down at the end of a dark deserted street. She would leave the safe lighted area and venture cautiously the dimly lit foreboding direction to her vehicle. She would reach halfway and then hear the footsteps behind her. Unable to run or scream she would wake up, her heart slamming against her chest. She once read that she should turn around in the dream and confront the owner of the footsteps, this being such an archetypal image, but she couldn't contain her fright to try anything.

Arturo wove his way through favorite partners and occasional strangers. He was well known in the Bay Area tango scene and many women sought him out. And there was always Letty.

"Have you tired already of your beautiful waitress?" Letty asked.

"She's hard to get to know. Maybe over time she'll warm up."

"But she wants to wait on your table now. Or do you want another twenty-year-old who's star struck with the great Arturo?"

"What makes you so sure that she's all that interested in me?"

"The way she checks me out to see if I'm romantic competition or not. And I can tell that you've enjoyed dancing more with her than anyone for a long time, except for me."

"And how did my psychic Leticia discern that?"

"Because you haven't looked this bothered at a dance in months." Arturo smiled uncomfortably, but didn't deny it. "And you know you've been keeping an eye on her since you last danced."

"It seems like I've met her before, but I can't place her."

"Really. You've been with so many women now that you forget them?"

"I don't know. I thought I would dance with her once more this evening and, if it goes well…"

"*Como no*, it will go well. *I juala!* Quit worrying—that's not the normal Arturo. Just be direct. It's ten minutes to midnight and soon they'll play "La Cumparsita" and the dance will be over. Better get in position and grab her or someone else will."

Olga was surprised to see Art standing near her and her partner as the song was nearing the end. He must want to dance with me again, she thought and felt the swelling rise in the belly of feeling wanted.

He broke in courteously before her current partner could whisk her off saying that he had promised her another dance—would he mind?

"I hope I wasn't rude, but I very much wanted to dance with you again."

"I'm glad you asked."

She had another chance. She sunk into his firm hold and would let her body speak. Why shouldn't she be with him? She could tell him what she wanted to. Maybe she could say that she attended clothing shows in Los Angeles, which was true, and not get caught by surprise at knowing too much about the big sprawling city down south.

Letty was right about Olga; she was not dancing shyly. A more sassy girl he would suspect of teasing or just flirting, but Olga was a serious woman and was sending a message. Still, pressing into him hardly meant she wanted to go home with him tonight. She would probably say yes to something casual later in the week. The last song came to a close. He held her in a tight embrace a little longer than would be normal and took a deep breath as he released her.

"Thank you. I'm glad that I at least got back to you for two more dances."

"I very much enjoyed dancing with you," Olga said.

She looked hauntingly familiar again. "Want to take a walk, perhaps something to drink?"

She agreed to the proposal. They gathered their things and exited into the abnormally warm San Francisco night. Leticia came up to them, gave Arturo a sisterly kiss and told Olga that it was great to meet her and that she looked forward to checking out her new clothes business. "You two look great together" were her last words as she walked off at a fast clip. Olga didn't appear to quite know how to take Leticia, Arturo thought, though she smiled back warmly. Then as she tilted her head to the side, Arturo started to form an eerie recognition, but he still couldn't place her. He had seen her before though, he was almost sure.

It wasn't the best ice breaker, but it was true, so he said it. "I keep thinking that I've met you before. Have you ever been to Los Angeles? Maybe we danced down there?"

Olga thought fast and tried to look calm. "I've been there a few times working, for my new online clothing business…and before, I was a clothes rep in Chicago and got to LA a few times. I went dancing once or twice."

"Do you remember which clubs?"

"No, it was a few years ago." She thought to change the subject, but he spoke again first.

"Was your hair longer then?" She couldn't believe this was happening. "Maybe a different color?"

"It was a little longer for a while. Maybe we danced once a few years ago…I really don't remember." She could see him searching his mind for a scene from almost four years ago. He must have been the detective, though she really couldn't swear to it herself. If he was going to place her, she would prefer to not be around when it happened. Maybe, if he did remember everything at some other time, he would realize to keep it to himself. This would be the test—that he never mention it, or only to her after a few months.

"Can we postpone getting a drink and I'll see you here dancing next week if not before?" she asked.

"I didn't mean to offend you," he said. "I really did think that I recognized you."

"No it's all right. It's late and I need to work tomorrow." She smiled at him, but her chest felt hollow. "Until next week?"

"Okay."

She turned in the direction of her car and started walking. Three men against a building stopped their conversation to look up and down the length of her short and tight dress. It had been a rare warm night and she hadn't brought her jacket. In the tango club, it was only an average outfit, but now on the street with strip clubs in both directions, she felt exposed. They kept staring. She heard steps behind her and then a voice.

"Olga, can I at least walk you to your car?" She felt his warm hand on her shoulder and turned towards the inviting voice. She liked the face she saw.

"That would be very nice." He put his arm softly on her back and they walked quietly. The offer by the man at the door of the strip club that "women get in for half price" sounded neither ominous nor familiar in the moment. Her car was only a few feet away.

Chapter 4

The Rewards

What You Get For Your Dedication

ANY DANCE FORM provides, at the very least, an opportunity for exercise. Cardiovascular, muscular exercise; balance, rhythmic, and strength training. Regular dancing provides it all and adds, besides, the elements of musicality and creativity. And social dancing adds the element of companionship, enlarging one's circle of friends, even the possibility of finding romance if one is looking for it.

While it offers all these things too, tango's uniqueness as a dance form extends, arguably, to some unique rewards. As tango gives up its secrets to its diligent students, they discover what tango has added to their lives. The spice and drama and sensuality of tango are qualities not to be underrated as are the regenerative possibilities to lives that have gone stale and marriages that could use a spark. We have seen lives given new lease by the pursuit of tango; notice we did not say the acquisition of tango. Once it is accepted that tango does not give up its secrets easily, then the pursuit of it becomes an ongoing project. So be it. The pursuit of a semi-mastery of tango—that is, a skill level that makes the dancer feel that he is an adequate leader or she a competent follower—is a goal that many have found to be reward in itself. Others give up once they find out how long this pursuit can go on.

But consider what prospective *tangueros*—who don't give up—get for their efforts: a dance that might make them feel young and sleek (no matter their poundage), seductive and desirable. A dance that encourages an emotional response to music, a dance that allows one's melancholy—whether an occasional or consistent personality trait—to find a hospitable home.

Do these rewards also, then, explain the motivation that brings a whole class of women to the tango floor? I'm thinking of those women who have non-dancing husbands or partners at home but who still passionately chase tango on their own, without their men. A number of tango professionals join us in puzzlement about this group. What is it that motivates them? Before I asked this question of women in this category, I took stock of my own assumptions. My first was that their life partners must have total confidence in themselves and in their relationship, confidence that the relationship wouldn't be threatened by the tango's intimacy. My second assumption was that these women are getting something from dancing tango that they don't get anywhere else in their lives, including from their primary relationship. It could be as simple and obvious as the enjoyment of moving to music they love, or as complex and subtle as the opportunity to live a secret, alter-life based on glamour and simulated romance. After all, no matter what the reality, dressing up, and going out to dance tango provides opportunities for a woman to get affirmation of her attractiveness and sex appeal; affirmation that she is still graceful and desirable, interesting, alive, and capable of re-creating herself.

My assumptions were fairly close to the truth, I found, once I started asking women about their motivations. One dancer gave her simple love of partner dancing as her prime reason, tango being the most challenging she's ever tried. Having urged her husband to join her in trying out different dances over the years, she finally gave up waiting for him and so they pursued their hobbies separately, with apparently no damage done to their marriage. "When men want adventure, they go climb mountains or take on a new sport. Women want to dance," said one woman in a similar marriage. I wonder, though, how many marriages are healthy enough to survive such disparate hobbies.

More frequently, the story behind a solo woman's appearance at milongas is couched in dissatisfaction with her overly-domestic marriage and the desire to escape it by reclaiming her feminine spirit and power. Obviously the setting for tango is the very antithesis of housewifery, so whatever the hubby thinks, these women are determined to have some innocent fun. They like the security of being married. At the same time they claim they like having what feels like a mini-affair without really cheating on their husbands and without entanglements. I have no trouble believing there are women who can sustain their marriages under these circumstances because I know some of them. On the other hand, there are others who may be fooling themselves. One *tanguera* friend warned: "a lot of women are looking for something more in their relationships, and a night out to a milonga or dance class is just the first step towards divorce. However, they may not know that at the time." Most people I talked to agree that it's easier for someone of either sex to fall in love on a dance floor than on a golf course or at a club meeting.

Still another blessing that some dancers claim is an almost spiritual experience that tango provides them, likening the movement to music in close embrace to a pure meditative state in which the practitioner's mind is wiped clear of any other "noise." Indeed, the best instructors often suggest that before taking the first step together, a couple should strive for stillness, both within and without. That might mean breathing deeply to find a place of breath coordination, also to calm the body and empty the mind.

Dancers, as they strive for the perfect "connection" that is their goal, must learn to relax in order to let that connection become possible, and then relax again into their partner's embrace so as to merge body and spirit. To trust, not only one's partner but also trust oneself to the moment and the music is the ultimate aim. When women dance with their eyes closed or cast down, what they are doing is submitting to the power of the moment and trusting their bodies will respond to the lead without their thinking about it. If I thought a friend's reminder to "shut up and dance" was just a jokey cliché, I now think differently about it. The best dancers I know dance their best when they "stay in the moment," which means not allowing their minds to go elsewhere. Some call it a "moving meditation."

It's not easy for a noisy brain like mine to meditate, but I can honestly say that the closest I've ever come to that state has occurred while wearing high heels and moving to the sounds of a bandoneon.

Closely related to tango's potential spiritual rewards are those that have to do with self-definition and energy balance. We've encountered some wonderful writing on that subject by Johanna Siegmann in *The Tao of Tango*. In this slim book, Johanna's intention is to relate a hypothesis she acquired through *living* her tango lessons. A self-described "female with male energy," always confused about relationships and mostly misunderstood by men, Johanna first experienced her female energy, for real, in the process of learning to tango. With great good humor, she shares her process of self-discovery and offers exercises and life lessons for the rest of us. Much more fun than the usual self-help book, *The Tao of Tango's* deceptively simple hypothesis draws an "aha!" kind of recognition from readers, who now know more about themselves and why they are so drawn to this phenomenon called tango.

> "I recall the epiphany I experienced with my very first step. All that fuzzy mumbo-jumbo about male-female, passive/aggressive suddenly crystallized. I knew what it all meant. I felt what it meant. I understood—mind, body, and soul—what it meant. I could see each clearly, independently of each other and their connection. And nothing else I had every done—no sport, class, art project, spiritual exercise—had even brought me close to this living, breathing knowledge. ...We as humans have been wired to require physical experience to understand intellectual concepts. No matter how many times you tell a child that fire will burn, "burn" has no meaning until it is experienced physically. Until you are able to experience the power of both male and female energy in yourself, you will be unable to respect and embrace them both." (Siegmann: 58)

Finally, there's the discovery that tango knows no age limits, a discovery that may add to one's willingness to pursue a new hobby late in age. It certainly did to mine, having taken my first lesson at age 58. That one can do a respectably competent tango in low gear and slow motion is obvious from attending any big city milonga where people of all ages gather. We love to watch the eighty-year-olds holding each other as closely and tenderly as the twenty-somethings. Older dancers may not wear their slit skirts as short or their tee shirts as tight across the chest, but they still look elegant in their simple black dresses and suits, cut soft and yielding for the leg movement that tango demands and which they are still able to perform, albeit modestly.

What's more, in the exquisite moments of a tango embrace, years can simply fall away. A couple sharing that embrace might lose all concept of time, age, place, and social barriers. In this next and last story, a highly unlikely couple break all the rules of convention in order to obey the inner truth of their hearts' voices.

"The Tango Embrace"

a story

"THIS COULD BE Argentina," Michael illustrated with a sweep of his hand, "balconies of old dark wood, heavy red curtains, and no one wearing jeans and T shirts."

"Have you been there?" asked Christine, whom he had just met on the dance floor.

"No" he smiled and lowered his gaze to her eyes, "this place just looks like the pictures I've seen."

"It is a beautiful club. Thank you for the dance. Maybe we'll dance again later?"

"I'll look forward to it." She strode away, slicing through the crowd with long carefully placed steps, another man swooping in to offer the next dance. Christine was still way above Michael's level, but he took satisfaction at now being able to, at least, keep the dance flowing through an entire song. Tango music and dance, conceived for passion and intimacy, had become the vehicle within which he could drive to the place he wanted to be, a woman's heart. Not any one woman, but all of them. In tango, he had found a way to reach beyond the time encumbering requirements of relating to women, avoiding the trappings of status and the protocols of conversation and embrace them with delight. Nothing he had encountered in his forty-five years was more beautiful.

He knew it was too early to tell whether he could carry the tango experience into the rest of his life with women. The dance of sexuality had, on occasion, followed from tango, but soon became challenged with the task of merging lives; the expenses of living in the same physical space and the limited time he had to give his lover after the demands of survival. Space and time, the old platforms of physics, seemed at odds with placing a man and woman together. Yet, in each tango, a three minute gift is offered to the dancers in which space and time are transcended; all of your time becomes your partner's and there isn't any space between you.

Michael returned to where he had left his glass of wine and leaned back against the wall. It was 10 o'clock and the place took on an air of excitement and anticipation. The best dancers were here and the beginners who had come early for the lesson hadn't left. Who to dance with next, he wondered. A woman walked in and paused by the door. He was first struck by her poise; she was calm and deliberate in her movements, watching the dancers with a peaceful appreciation. She was older than most, or maybe all of the dancers, well into her sixties, he figured. Tango didn't tend to draw a young crowd, like swing, but most of the tango dancers in the United States were in their thirties, forties, and fifties. She took off her jacket and made her way to the coatroom. In doing so she walked right past him—tall, with active eyes which tried to take in everything. She caught his gaze and offered a comfortable and relaxed smile. Returning from the coatroom, she took a place standing near the edge of the dance floor. Guessing that she was a highly experienced dancer, he decided to ask her first before any of the best leaders did and set a standard with her for the night.

"Hi, I'm Michael, would you like to dance?"

She turned towards him and answered without hesitation, "I would love to."

Both her face up close and the feel of her body were of a woman near seventy; although her posture was erect, her frame had a slight rigidity of exposed bones, lacking the extra flesh of thin younger women. She stepped back gracefully though and it was obvious that he was right about her dance experience. Her height, only three or four inches less than his, made the close dance position easy to assume and she cradled lightly in his arms. They flowed smoothly through basic patterns around the room. He sensed her age in her steps, graceful and sure, but with occasional faltering shifts, as she seemed to favor some weak area. Still, it was a pleasure to dance with her. When the dance ended she said, "Sorry, I haven't danced in a while and I'm a little stiff."

He was taken aback by an apology and responded quickly, "No, you danced beautifully. I'm new at this myself. You probably mistook beginner's uncertainty for attempts at highly skilled maneuvers. In fact, would you dance with me again before one of the advanced dancers snatches you up and you realize that all mix-ups were my fault all along?"

He offered his arms in dance position and she settled in once again, only this time a little closer, with her chest barely resting against his. The tango embrace, unlike any of the other formal dances he had tried, allowed, no, intentionally created this beautiful place for a man and woman to hold each other in the safety, passion, and mystery of a greater dance. They danced slowly. He carefully placed her feet securely for each step, omitting all flashy movements meant more for the impressing of onlookers than the dancers themselves. All that mattered to him was that he kept the dance safely moving so that this magnificent warmth nestled in his arms would stay there. When the song ended, without breaking the hold, he simply whispered, "Another?" close to her ear. "Please," he heard her say. The next song was faster and he half timed a lot of steps to avoid the need to create distance between them. During a rather dynamic instrumental solo he attempted one faster combination as inspired by the music and whether by his imprecise lead or some lack on her part, she stumbled. He had such a strong hold on her she couldn't go far and she caught her balance quickly.

"Sorry, my fault. Are you okay?"

"It was me, I strained a muscle in my right foot and it twinges occasionally. I'm fine." The tightened muscles in her face didn't resonate the same certainty.

He placed her even more carefully on each step. The song ended, the last in that set, as is the pattern in tango milongas; several songs are played, frequently of a similar style and then there's a very short interlude of non-tango music called the *cortina*, meaning curtain, while dancers reshuffle.

"Can I get you a drink?"

"It's wonderful of you to ask. Red wine would be fine."

He led her to a table and brought back a glass of wine. "I'm Rita," she offered and held out her hand, combined with a smile he knew he could become addicted to.

"Michael." He took her hand and then squeezed it with both hands. "I haven't seen you dancing in the Bay Area before, but you're obviously an experienced dancer. Where do you dance normally?" It wasn't as well phrased as he would have liked, not wanting to imply "age" to the question.

"Most of my dancing has been in Argentina. I was born here, in San Francisco, but lived the last fifty years in Buenos Aires. I used to dance every week for a long time." She paused and the emotional well rose to her surface and subsided before cresting the wall as tears. Michael looked on uncertain whether to change the subject, though he wanted to know who she was. "My husband died almost two years ago and I haven't danced since."

"I'm sorry to hear that," he offered and she smiled weakly. "Was your husband Argentinean?"

"Yes."

"How did you meet? Am I being too forward?"

"No, not at all. Carlos, my husband, ended up in San Francisco during the war through a rather complicated turn of events regarding his family's shipping industry and due to Argentina's rather precarious position in the war. He stayed here most of the war and a couple of years after. I was just finishing high school when we met, he was nearly ten years older than me, and he charmed me into his heart within days." She paused, looked up at Michael and continued. "Carlos taught me to dance, as you probably guessed. There wasn't much tango in the States then. We lived in the U.S. for a while, but political pressures made it hard to continue business here so we moved to Argentina, much to the horror of my parents."

"Were you here visiting them?"

"No, they've been gone a long time. My brother died a few months ago, which is what brought me back to San Francisco. I even thought about moving back here. My daughter married a Spaniard and lives in Barcelona, probably some form of just revenge from my parents. My son makes his home in Buenos Aires, but he travels frequently.

Things seem to be changing faster all the time." A song ended and Rita waited through the short break until the next one began. "I had considered moving back here, but everyone I knew has either left or I've lost track of them. It's not home and it would take more energy than I want to spend to make it so. I chose Argentina a long time ago and it's too late to uproot myself again. I'm flying back in the morning. This seemed like an appropriate last night in San Francisco. I probably told you more than you were after."

"No, not at all. I was simply overwhelmed trying to take in what I'm sure was an incredibly rich and complex life in three minutes. Thank you for telling me. These last couple of years must have been very hard for you."

"Yes. I had a lot of support in the beginning, after Carlos died, but other people have their own lives and I've been searching for what my life can be living alone again after all these years. I had to return here to see that Argentina is my home."

"Let's dance again."

"But I've done all the talking and you haven't told me anything about yourself."

"I'm a forty-five year old California native, employed in a field I enjoy, recently divorced, no kids, and I love to dance more than anything else. And I've just met a fascinating and beautiful woman who's spending her last night in the United States and I would much rather dance with her than labor through the comparatively mundane story of my life." She offered her hand. And as they danced, she offered her body, letting her chest rest against his even while she supported herself. They danced several songs, without speaking in between. His arm around her back and her long fingers draped across his hand completed the blessed connection. He took in the sweet almond-like aroma from her hair with every breath.

After this set of songs, he walked her back to the table and excused himself to the restroom. When he returned through the dark side rooms and corridors, she was dancing with one of the many teachers that frequent the club. Although all the old voices of inadequacy vied for attention as he watched a master of the dance execute his flawless style on a woman he had rapidly grown fond of, he also found great pleasure in watching her move. Like any good dancer, her current partner quickly realized her favored leg and conformed the dance to her needs. Still, they looked marvelous together and he made her shine. That wasn't hard to do, he told himself. She must have been stunning in her youth. He sighed to himself with the realization that she still was. Of course. He had unconsciously told himself that she was seventy and therefore how could he find her so attractive. But he did. How could anyone honestly see her and not? She had kept herself supple and thin. Her hair was carefully styled to frame her face, probably dyed to the dark brunette of her youth. It was her face, though, highlighted by bright dark eyes, that ultimately held his attention. She looked her age, yet she didn't seem of his parent's generation. He simply saw a beautiful woman who was a lot older than he was. He knew then that he wanted to spend this night with her, her last in the country.

She danced two songs with her current partner and then they talked for a moment before he escorted her back to the table where Michael waited. It dawned on him that their positioning together at a small table gave the appearance that they were somehow a couple. They thanked each other and Rita sat down and turned towards Michael. "I had forgotten how much dancing tango does for me."

"You both looked wonderful out there. Is it all right that I share your table?"

"I thought I was sharing yours. Either way, yes," and she lightly placed her hand on his and then, just as quickly, pulled it away with a trace of awkwardness in her expression, hoping, Michael figured, that neither gesture was inappropriate. After a sip of wine, she looked at him again, "I know he is an instructor and a great dancer, but I actually enjoy dancing with you more."

Her gaze shifted nervously from Michael to arbitrary points around the room. Had their ages somehow been closer, he knew he would be starting a campaign to keep her from ever boarding another plane without him. He thought of telling her how beautiful she was, but it sounded potentially embarrassing in the moment; he wouldn't have said this to a younger woman so early in an encounter. Feelings never come with labels, words have to be applied until their sound matches them and hopefully, they match for the other person as well. What he said was, "I've lost all interest in dancing with anyone else tonight."

She stepped deep into his embrace without shyness. They danced several songs at a time the rest of the evening, taking only short breaks to rest their feet and sip wine. Since it was a Sunday, the club closed at midnight. The last dance was announced and the familiar melody of *La Cumparsita* filled the room. Michael had noticed early on in tango that the evening always seemed to last a long time, in spite of the fact that he found so much enjoyment in it. Tango appeared to have the ability to bend time. Tonight was an extreme example of this; he had only known her a little over two hours, but because he knew her in tango, they had reached deep inside the other to a place that usually requires months. They held each other securely through the last song until the music stopped. He released her slowly and she said, "I have had such a wonderful time tonight. Thank you so much!"

"Thank *you*." He hesitated and then asked, "Will you spend the night with me?"

She blushed and looked at once both pleased and anxious. She looked deeper into his eyes and then away and didn't answer. Returning her gaze she said, "It's very nice of you to ask."

"I'm not asking to be nice."

"I know" and she squeezed his arms. "I know." They stared at each other. Across her face flickered every age she had been in Michael's imagination. He hoped that his request didn't cause her any pain or misgiving, but he wanted to be with her on this last night.

"It would be enough to just hold you until dawn," he added. Her face filled with gratitude and she pressed against him, squeezed tight for a few seconds, took a deep breath, and released.

"I'm going to say no to you and I don't have a rational reason. I just can't bear any awkwardness spoiling what we have right now."

"I don't have any sexual agenda."

"I know," and she touched his cheek and mouth "please accept what I'm saying." The pleading in her eyes kept him from asking any more. "There is one thing that you could do that would mean a tremendous amount to me. Would you take me back to my hotel room and escort me to the airport in the morning? I know this is a lot to ask, especially since I'm not letting you stay the night with me. Don't say yes unless it feels right."

People passed in back of them. He heard several good-byes spoken. "OK, I'd be glad to." Maybe, as he walked her to her room, she would change her mind, he thought. They got their coats and stepped outside of the sacred space of the dance floor framed by the small round tables. Michael felt the shift even as he held her arm and they descended the stairs to the noisy street below; the shift in his confidence and the shift in his knowledge, for the positions and patterns off the dance floor were so much harder to discern. The woman at his side maintained her poise and offered her genuine smile on demand, a trait which must still give her away as American in her home of Argentina. She also looked vulnerable and alone, though he wondered if the latter was just a reflection of himself. He knew it was arrogant and unfair to think that she should be saying yes to his request because he was much younger than she was. He would have to trust her that being in bed together would be hard or even painful for her. Alas, he knew very little about her, what she needed, or what she hoped for.

"It's all right if you're a little angry with me. I am flattered that a young handsome man wants me. It's also more than I can take on emotionally right now. But don't think that me wanting to have you take me to the airport is any sort of consolation offering—I want your company now and tomorrow morning very much."

They were walking with her arm tucked in his. He looked down into her eyes and saw a perpetual gentle fire and a longing that no one was going to fill in one night. He was struck by the image of her holding Carlos' arm in the same way she had his now as they walked down these same streets fifty years before. Michael realized he was envious of an opportunity that had passed a few years before he was even born. "I'm not at all angry with you, Rita. I'm just jealous that Carlos had all those years with you instead of me! Tell me that isn't silly. But I am happy to know that you were loved. I feel like God mixed up our birth dates somehow."

Rita broke into a laugh, a short sob, and then radiated her smile once more. He put his arm around her and they walked in a now comfortable silence to the car and he drove her to the downtown hotel.

"Even though there are so many new buildings and more people, San Francisco has an odd way of looking like it did fifty years ago because the hills are still the same," Rita spoke softly while watching the city through the passenger window. She looked over at Michael with words forming on her lips, but she didn't say them. Michael noticed and started to encourage her and then refrained himself. They arrived at the hotel and he parked in the twenty-minute zone. She didn't wait for him to open her door for her, but did take his arm. They walked through the lobby towards the elevators. The night desk clerk darted his eyes back and forth between them and then nodded a salutation. At the elevator Rita turned towards him, took his face with both hands and said, "You've given me as wonderful of evening as I could have hoped for" and kissed him on the lips. She stared into his eyes for a moment, said good night, abruptly turned and entered the elevator.

"Good night, Rita. I'll be here at seven for you." She returned an oddly shy wave and the door closed.

No one was around, so he watched the elevator ascend to the fourth floor and stop. And there it stayed. Michael turned and headed for the door. The desk clerk offered a chipper good night. The car door shut with a hollow thunk and he started across the bay for home. He wondered if her decision to spend the night alone reflected their difference in age. Was such an intense short-term encounter less appealing to an older person? Would she have accepted the offer from a man closer to her age who she might expect a better chance of a long-term relationship? In honesty, she was likely too old for him to commit himself to, though he wasn't sure. Had her story been that she was moving back to San Francisco, would he have invited her for this night? Probably not. But he would have seen her again and they would have danced. He could still feel the electric-like connection from her touch.

He set the alarm for 6:00 realizing that this would be a short night.

He lay on his back thinking of the gossip they would create, the unsure reaction of friends and family, of how people would always be "wondering" when they saw them together. Suddenly, he felt emotionally very tired.

Michael's dependable inner clock aroused him at five minutes to six. He turned off the alarm before it sounded and got up. Traffic was still light at this hour and he arrived at the hotel twenty minutes early. He parked and hurried inside deciding that he would surprise her at the door of her room allowing ten minutes in private. "Excuse me, I forget Ms. Rita Mendez' room number on the fourth floor."

"Would you like for me to call her room and say that you're here?"

"No, I'd like to surprise her. I just need the room number."

"I'm sorry, but it's our hotel policy not to give out room numbers without permission. I would be happy to call her and..." Just then, Rita turned the corner by the elevators with a valet and her bags.

Rita hadn't noticed him yet and he approached slowly. From fifty feet she looked his peer. At fifteen feet he stopped and let her finish with the valet. Her face danced in the conversation, a smile lifting her face into youth and then settling back again to show her years. Was this the second of two days he would ever spend with this woman? Both days holding a mere three hours at that. Tango wasn't for the weak of heart, he thought to himself. Rita tipped the valet, saw Michael, and broke into a grin.

"Good morning, Rita."

"This was the longest short night I can remember. I guess that's what happens when you can't sleep and you're not with the one you're thinking about. Of course, I was the orchestrator of that." She took both of his hands and said, "Thank you for being here now."

He drew her in to his chest and squeezed tightly. "I wonder what would be different right now if I would have spent the night with you?"

She responded with silence and eyes that no longer focused on him. Michael spoke again, "You don't need to say anything. I just wanted you to know what's going on in my own head. Let's get to the airport before traffic picks up."

During the drive to the airport she kept a constant string of questions running about his early years and his parents, college, work, and friends. He wondered how much she really wanted to know, thinking that perhaps, instead, she wanted to avoid nervous silence or more troubling questions that he might spring. What he wanted to do was to dance a never ending tango with her.

"I didn't ask you what time you needed to be at work," she inquired with a tone of urgency as they made their way in from the parking lot. "I don't want to make you late. If you need to…"

He interrupted, "It's all right. My schedule today is flexible. I'd like to stay with you until you leave."

"If that's really okay, yes." They were without steps, patterns, and convention. They didn't even have a dance position to fall back on. What did he want? Oh, he knew what he wanted, but the fantasy of her being twenty or thirty years younger wasn't aiding him. The truth was, given the reality of their ages, he didn't know what he wanted. If she suddenly turned and said she wanted to postpone her flight for a week so that they could be together, it would have caused as much anxiety as joy. For her to see that in him made his gut churn. He guessed that what he wanted most was a warm and friendly parting appropriate to the dear connection that they had last night. With this thought he looked towards her, only to find her eyes already on him with an expression of longing that needed his attention. He took her hand and held it against the side of his chest. Better. She took a deep breath and the line moved forward.

With the baggage checked, he could put his arm around her as they made their way to the gate. Michael accepted the steady clatter of suitcase wheels and hum of voices as a release from trying to speak. Rita nestled in his arm and they found a place of comfort. After all, he thought, it was the embrace last evening that allowed them to be so close. All he wanted last night was to continue the embrace, but even that was not so simple. He would do what he could now to make this woman feel appreciated and cared for. They came to the gate and stopped. Michael gazed down the line of black chairs, attached in rows facing other rows. He knew in an instant that sitting for an hour side by side with arm rests between them and on display would be hell. He looked around and saw an open area in the corner near the phones.

"Let's go over by the windows," he said. They came to the large glass picture window and stood looking out upon the docked jets and runways, his arm still around her. He turned her towards him and they stood only a few inches apart.

Michael knew he had to lead something and the illusion to dance would have been humorous if not for the confused expression on the woman in front of him. Without thinking, Michael slipped his right arm around her back and took her right hand in his left and raised it to a tango hold. Her confusion was replaced by amazement and Michael himself didn't know what he was going to do next. He drew her against him, encircled her arms around him, laid her head on his chest, and wrapped both arms around her. He nestled his face into her hair and held tightly. This was what he wanted, to hold her close. Maybe she wanted something else. It was the most honest expression he could give, just hugging her. She was still and didn't struggle, but he could feel a tension in her. Michael was aware of being watched by a woman at the telephone and a couple sitting twenty feet away. He held Rita firmly and carefully. He didn't press hard anywhere, but he was aware of every point of contact, from his fingers and palms spread wide against her back, along his forearms through his biceps, and the front of his thighs against hers. He spoke to her with his body and he waited for an answer. She shifted her arms against his back, but he didn't lighten his hold. Her shoulders softened and then gave and she surrendered her chest into his. Now he was aware of her breath as her small breasts and belly would rise into him slightly and then retreat. He closed his eyes and sank against the top of her head. His hip had the window wall to lean on for stability and he used it for an anchor. The rest of his body he gave to Rita and she accepted. With his eyes closed, he was aware of all the boarding announcements—Mexico City, Rio, Pa'pete. Rita's breathing became irregular and he could feel small sobs vibrate from her chest to his. Then the sobs subsided into sniffs and she relaxed her entire body into his. He began to gently rub the fingers of his right hand against her upper back, although careful not to in any way release the tight grip of his arms. He didn't want her to move, only to feel.

Michael kept deliberate connection to her from his fingers to his legs. Had she struggled at all to end the embrace he would have, of course, let her, but she didn't attempt any movement. She leaned into him without resistance and stayed there nuzzled in as if she could go to sleep. No words came to him that were worth breaking the hold. They stood, wrapped around each other as completely as they could be while standing and Michael had no plan to let go. The impending flight to Argentina faded into a dreamscape much like when a person half awakens before the alarm has gone off, not checking whether it will ring in one minute or one hour and drifting in slumber through unknown time. He felt gratitude for tango, which opened the place for this to happen. Like the tango dance itself, there wasn't anything easy about what they were sharing.

"At this time we would like to start boarding for flight number 934. All first class passengers and passengers needing assistance should proceed to the gate and prepare to board..."

Rita stirred in his arms and slowly raised her eyes to his. She did indeed look like someone who had just woken up. Her eyes glistened with the tears that hadn't quite dried. "Thank you," she said. "That was one of the most beautiful moments of my life."

"Are you a good letter writer?" she continued.

"I guess so. I mean I used to be. Nowadays I usually send emails."

"It would mean a tremendous amount if you wrote to me. And not emails, but hand written letters. I want to see as much of you in them as I can. I'll respond to every letter right away, I promise. Write about anything; your work, your friends, stories, what troubles you, what brings you joy—anything, anything at all—as often as you like. You have no idea how much this would mean to me."

But he did. He saw the exuberant girl, the ravishing young woman, the mature loving woman, and the wise, deeply generous and caring woman all speaking from within a lovely aged body. She knew exactly what their relationship needed and he felt dumbstruck at the obvious course that hadn't even crossed his mind. He took her face in both hands and gave her a long kiss on the lips. She took him in and let him finish. "I'll write you today" he paused, "and I'll write you often."

Her emotions welled up, but she didn't cry. Instead, her face beamed at him a bright and painful light. She swallowed and took a deep breath. "We may never see each other again." She hesitated. "I don't know. But if I keep receiving letters from you, I'll never lose you. Maybe we'll see each other after a while. Here's my address." She took out a pen and paper and wrote them down.

They waited together twenty feet from the gate until the line had filed into the plane. They stood face to face in a loose embrace. "It was a very difficult decision last night for me to say no to your offer. I lay awake alternating between feeling like a fool and being relieved. Even now, I don't know if I made the best decision. Though, I do know that this morning couldn't have been better." Michael reached up and softly stroked her face. She looked pleased. He was very glad for her steadiness at that moment. "Isn't age a funny thing?" she spoke softly with no change of expression.

Michael smiled lightly, but inside he wanted to scream—a scream without words. "I feel like a dancer who suddenly can't remember a damn step and I stumble into my partner in the middle of the floor."

"You're dancing beautifully to the music and your partner is very happy."

"Last boarding call for flight 934. All passengers report at once…"

He gave her a quick kiss and then squeezed her a last time. *"Vaya con paz y amor, Carina mia."*

"You speak Spanish!" she exclaimed and broke into a huge grin. "Write me!" she shouted after giving her boarding pass.

The airline personnel looked entertained, but he had no wish to engage them with a response. Instead, he walked over to the last chair by the window and sat down. Breathing deeply for the first time all morning, he stared at the jet as they closed the doors and taxied back. He was amazed to see that one of his strongest feelings was relief. He realized just how afraid he was of hurting her with his

uncertainty over their age difference. Maybe he had danced well to
the music. Looking down, he saw the paper with her address in his
hand. This was their only connection now. She didn't even know
his last name. He folded the paper carefully and buttoned it into his
shirt pocket.

Michael enjoyed every step retracing his way back through the
terminal. He felt vibrantly alive, acutely aware and oddly interested
in the expressions and lives of the strangers passing by. Rita was
still imprinted into his flesh like fabric that creases the skin. How
horrible he might have felt right now without her address. What
a magician she had been with the intent of letters. Would he ever
see her again? Would they write every week for a year and then
meet again? Who would they be then? Close friends? Would they
ever be lovers? Had they already been in this timeless evening and
morning? He would most certainly be with other women before he
saw Rita again. He wanted Rita to be with a man and he hoped to
hell that whoever it was appreciated her. Michael took this as an odd
thought to have. Would he want another man to be with a woman
he wanted for himself as a lover? Maybe what he felt was something
beyond a jealous, territorial love. He noticed how much enjoyment
he was getting from watching the hundreds of women flow past
him; women of all ages and looks, women he wanted to tango with.
He wanted to embrace them. Some he would want to hold on to
longer than others. What an amazing dance it was.

Finally, after a whirlwind of activity at the office, he sat down in
his apartment with his take-out Thai and several sheets of unlined
hand crafted paper. He was staggered at the thought that twenty-four
hours ago he hadn't even met Rita. In spite of his physical exhaustion,
he still felt vibrantly alive. The blank pages looked daunting, but he
was going to mail her a letter tomorrow morning. There was no
question about this. He could see that the first letter was definitely
the hardest, assuming there was no last. It had been the convention
of the dance though for him to take the lead.

"*Carina mia,*

Last night I met the most fabulous woman. Let me tell you about
her…"

Building A Tango Community

If you have discovered it on your own and you live in an area where tango is not yet a fixture, you have no doubt thought about turning on your friends and potential friends to tango, so that a community might result. Having a tango community nearby offers all kinds of ultimate rewards, not the least of which are the fun of sharing a creative passion with other people, having more partners to dance with, parties and more parties.

Once you've interested at least a dozen people, the most important first step is to invite teachers to your community to hold a workshop or series of workshops in beginning level tango. Recommendations for teachers are best gotten by word of mouth, we've found. Find out which teachers have been useful to beginning groups in other communities like yours. Most likely they will have a web-site with information you can download and share with your target audience — the email addresses you might have gathered from your local dance studio, to start.

Several groups we know began by inviting some well-known teachers to do a performance in their community followed by a beginning lesson and information session. Sign ups, then, for more information about future lessons could be ideally promoted in such a setting. Once you have a group who've had a few lessons, you can think about instituting regular *practica* sessions, especially if more experienced dancers agree to do some casual coaching along the way.

But here's the caveat: *there is no substitute for formal and consistent instruction.* Any group members serious about learning tango and building their community *must* not only bring in teachers regularly but also urge their friends to seek instruction elsewhere... at workshops in other cities or dance camps.

The sad alternative is that most members do not progress, or get discouraged, so that they never reach that level of fulfillment required to stay with tango. And the more experienced members looking for new partners are inevitably disappointed too. It's already a challenge to keep together a group of people with wildly different experience levels. That's why we offer the caveat. Once it's agreed upon that instruction is a goal communally "owned," go into your project with enthusiasm and determination to grow your group successfully.

The U.S. Tango Trail

Once you're reasonably sure that you've passed beyond the beginning level, you're ready to get the most from exploring the "tango trail." This is what we call the series of adventures offered by tango-event organizers around the U.S. and elsewhere. Some of these we've mentioned in earlier chapters but are worth mentioning again. A few others are mentioned in Appendix 1.

Attending one of these camps for grown-up dance students is a treat on so many levels that we can recommend it highly as part of the tango experience. The only people we've encountered who have been disappointed or unduly frustrated by their camp experience are those who simply weren't quite ready for it. A beginner who consistently finds himself or herself the least accomplished in a group class, no matter how high his enthusiasm, is bound to suffer wounded self-esteem, enough even to doubt his ability to continue. An additional set of group or private lessons specifically geared to beginners—taken before taking on an intense camp—might have saved him this painful disappointment. It's always a good idea to ask your teacher for an opinion about your readiness for dance camp.

Most people, we've found, come away from a tango camp feeling renewed, inspired, refreshed, committed to dancing ever more seriously and more often. Even those who report feeling frustrated and discouraged by their slow progress nonetheless pledge to attend the next one and try harder! If you travel often on business or for other reasons, you have still other alternatives. Always a smart thing to do is check out the tango scene that exists wherever you're going by doing a web search. We've found that *Tango+ Destination City* brings up all the information you'll need to find out what's happening in that area.

Typically, for a camp or tango festival, you are expected to buy a package which includes instruction and nightly milongas. Meals and hotel are generally paid for separately. You can expect to pay $100-150 per day for 4-5 hours of instruction plus evening milonga. (A separate charge for milongas may be required when the music is live.) Often you are offered private lessons as well, at a separate rate per hour. Camp organizers used to allow you to make a videotape to take home with you; typically the instructors would demonstrate the lesson's subject and give people a chance to video that for practice purposes. Today, only a few camps allow this practice and charge a fee for a "video permit." More common today is for a professional videographer to make a video of all the instructional sessions and then sell it to attendees at the end, an option we find much less valuable than the homemade variety.

The most expensive camps are those in which the instructional staff come from the highest echelon of Argentine dancers. The value of having such instructors lies primarily in the authenticity they bring to the tango experience and the excitement and inspiration they generate for the dance. Not to be missed are the wonderfully colorful stories they tell about their beginnings as *porteños, tangueros,* and as performers around the world. You can read some interviews with stars in *Paul Pellicoro on Tango.* (See references page for details.)

But the rewards of tango camps go far beyond the style, skill, and inspiration modeled and practiced by the *maestros*. The workshop sessions are fine places to meet new people who share your tango passion. See Appendix I for a list of tango camps and festivals in the U. S. as well as international tango resources.

The Tango Toolkit

Oh, the many temptations of tango. Beyond the delicious dance itself, there are the attractive trips that ambitious teachers and travel agents organize around dance instruction, so that you can mix pleasure with pleasure. And beyond even the trips is the temptation to grow a glamorous wardrobe. Sally Potter showed us how in "The Tango Lesson" when she tried on her first pair of four inch heels, amused and pleased at how she looked no matter how uncomfortable she felt. Women everywhere normally devoted to Birkenstocks and corduroy discover they like satin and fringe and fishnet stockings. So do their partners. Dressing up this way for the first time is easier when you're far from home and can be anyone you want. Go for it, we say.

As we pack for another tango camp, I'm going through the usual craziness of indecision. We're flying this time and therefore don't want to over-pack, but what to leave out? I want to take clothes that are attractive but also dance-able—that means comfortable, cool, light weight, and at least somewhat "glam." Deciding upon which items are the indispensables for a four day camp usually turns up a list like the following.

For classes: one pair of my favorite slimming, elasticized black pants (something every middle aged woman should own) with two appropriate tops; one short skirt with slit and two tops. Tops, for me, are either sleeveless and shiny or if with sleeves, they are silky and cool. One pair low heeled, sensible practice shoes and one pair dance sneakers (ugly but they might make the difference between dropping out early and lasting the whole day.) These are available from Capezio and from Bloch.

Comfort items: shoe pads, talcum powder, refreezable icebag that can be carried to class in a small cooler (for icing feet that are prone to swelling or pain), arnica gel or tiger balm for sore muscles. Energy bars for a quick snack, or for when there isn't quite enough time for lunch between sessions. Be prepared to buy a quart of good water per day to carry around with you during sessions.

For milongas: four different outfits because milongas take a heavy toll in wear and perspiration. Two of these could be built around one skirt and two tops; the other two, dresses. Tango clothes are fun and women usually take advantage of the opportunity to dress up in short or long dresses with fringes, slits, uneven hems, floaty fabrics, long sparkly earrings and other jewelry. The favorite colors are black and red. Preferred shoes are strappy shoes designed especially for tango, with the highest heels a dancer can tolerate. (See the Appendix for recommended shoe dealers.)

Men's clothes decisions, as usual, don't cause as much trouble or take as much space in a suitcase. For practice and classes, men wear anything that's comfortable, other than shorts. For milongas men wear soft suits, silk or tropical shirts or dressy well-fitting tee shirts and often tapered pants, and shoes designed for dancers. Young *tangueros* devoted to new generation style, as we've mentioned, might turn up in cargo pants with a tee shirt under an open dress shirt.

Other accessories: we like to carry a flask of brandy for a nightcap. American dancers tend not to drink much or at all during dances, knowing that alcohol will affect performance on the floor, so it's nice to have that nip available for afterward, no matter where you are.

The Future of Tango

Robert Duvall, in his National Geographic special on Argentine tango, raised the questions "where will tango go from here? Will it survive?" We thought his lugubriously expressed concern a bit overstated considering the popularity and resilience of tango as a dance form in this century. But now that we've become tango-watchers as well as tango dancers, we're beginning to see that tango as we know it *could* indeed evolve into something having several new branches, the more sedate style called "salon" becoming perhaps the form retained by the older generation only, somewhat parallel to the way foxtrot survives, or East coast swing. Among the younger set, such dances as these are practiced only as self-consciously retro, even antique, while greater numbers of their peers are dancing to rhythms dictated by the moment's pop music. It's not unreasonable to foresee that same future for tango.

Meanwhile the dance form that's called *tango nuevo* or "new generation tango" is catching on lately—at least on the West Coast—with a speed that we wouldn't have predicted a year ago. Friends who attended a popular tango camp in the summer of '02 reported that a young instructor, called in at the last moment to replace a no-show instructor, generated such heat with his new generation style that his workshops drew the largest groups of dancers and were the subject of enthusiastic talk everywhere dancers gathered. The gist of this talk, our friends reported, suggested that young dancers found the classical salon style, usually dominating the instruction at such camps, to be a bit stodgy, compared to *tango nuevo* and *milonguero* styles. We predict that all current styles will stay alive to some degree, though splitting along the generational lines over time.

And what might a "pop" version of tango music sound like? The imagination boggles at the possibilities. So-called "extreme tango" sounds could be called a fusion with rock, as in "The Gotan Project." Of course, that both tango music and dance are said to have originated as fusion forms, earning their common label as Creole forms (*criolla*) points to the distinct possibility that fusion lies ahead for the future of tango as well. We've already mentioned the emergence of slango and swango in some circles. And there's "world music," as one imaginable analog. World music, that hybridized genre including fusions of Afro, Latin, Middle Eastern, and American pop, backed by acoustic drumming or electronic beat. Knowing that world music is multiculturally and politically correct, I dislike it even more. Bland and faceless, it could signal — with a wild stretch of the imagination — the future of tango music once it's melded with samba or techno, or some yet unknown pop music to produce a mongrel that pales next to the tango forms that we know. But then again, people hated Piazzolla's *tango nuevo* too as a "violation" of tango.

Rather, we're guessing that Argentine tango's history, relatively complex compared to the fairly linear history of other partner dance styles, necessarily complicates any effort to predict its future. Nor is Argentine tango at all like the codified American and International tango, which are kept from evolving by their very codes. On the other hand, being a creolized dance doesn't necessarily doom it, either, to continually evolving creolization. Look at other musical and dance creoles which have more or less stopped in their tracks: Cubano son and bolero, cajun, Celtic fiddle, American bluegrass, Dixieland jazz, samba, mambo — all of them remaining consistent and unique from decade to decade.

For now, fusion in the future or not, we'll continue to enjoy the limited diversity of tango music most favored by dancers: folksy milongas and lively waltzes from the earliest collections, steady beats from the *orquesta tipica* heydays, the inventiveness of Pugliese, languorous novelties such as the poignant harmonica of Hugo Diaz, and of course Piazzolla arrangements, now considered danceable even though Piazolla never intended them to be. As long as the music has fire and heat, bite and beat, and preferably a bandoneon wailing from out of imagined darkness, it can be danced.

And danced, it will be. We can't imagine a time when tango and its *afficionados* might no longer be a part of the dancing landscape. As I write this, *Forever Tango* is announced as "held over for another four weeks" in San Francisco. No doubt, next year a new tango show will open in Buenos Aires or on Broadway, and another the year after that. And while there may always be more people who want to listen to tango music and watch tango performed than to dance it, the draw of tango as a social dance won't go away any time soon.

Why? If you are still asking this question at the end of this book, it may be because you have tried to understand tango in a rational way. Tango's mysteries, however, don't reveal themselves through reason. "Why are these people so crazy about tango," you ask? Because tango drives its acolytes crazy! And feeling a bit crazy is part of its spell. You have to utterly fall under its spell, go a bit nuts for your next "fix" so as to manage your addiction, in order to come close to understanding why so many people become obsessed with tango. Then, too, you have to be willing to have your heart broken now and then. Tango music, to begin with, not only makes a heart race but makes a heart break with its poignancy and implied suffering. And, trust me, the learner's heart will break again and again with disappointment over not dancing well enough or not attracting a certain dancer or not having a steady partner to share the magic with. There's plenty of pain on the way to the pleasure of tango.

When we say that the intimacy afforded by tango can be more satisfying than sex, it may be because sexual hunger is, for many, easier to satisfy than the yearning for intimacy that lies at tango's origin and which keeps people coming back, decade after decade.

Contemporary life, lived-out through the media and on the street and in our homes and workplaces, does not necessarily provide or promote the kind of intimacy that we human beings seem to crave. Meanwhile, from the moment an experienced couple join in a tango embrace and surrender to its demand for mutual trust and respect they are, in essence, shutting out the rest of the world and creating their own, a world perhaps visited only briefly, but well-worth all the shoe-leather spent to arrive there.

We conclude these musings on the future of tango with my co-author's, Larry's, description of an all-night milonga that for him had all the "fire and heat, bite and beat" to make it his most memorable to that point. Wherever tango's future lies, he wants *his* future to be full of nights like this.

A Milonga to Remember—or Last Milonga in Portland

A live tango orchestra, what a treat—bandoneon, piano, violin, and bass— was underway by 8:30. Dancing to a talented live orchestra is much richer than to recorded music; dancers and musicians inspire each other to taste heartily of the perfect moment. We arrived shortly after the band started, amazed at the empty space on the floor. Beginners outnumbered advanced dancers about two to one. While space allowed, I tried many of the new steps we had been introduced to in the classes of the week.

By 9:30 the floor was packed. Close embrace was now the dominant style. Beginners drifted off the floor to watch the advanced dancers, many of them teachers. Nothing compares with the build-up for the big-night event. The finest outfits are donned; pin-striped vests with double-breasted coats, sleek black dresses with dangling fringes like a curtain to an inner room. Eyes are wide open. Hugs, kisses, and last dances for another year. The volume builds and we are lifted along on a wave of sound and sensuality.

The Show. The band sets down their instruments while the rest of us seek out a place to observe. We sit on the floor setting the boundaries, line the walls, fill the stairs—anywhere that offers a view and affords comfort for the hour. Then the teachers perform a wide variety of exhibitions ranging from startlingly simple renditions danced with such elegance, like the perfect Gravenstein apple plucked at its hour of perfection on a thirsty August afternoon, to exhilarating tangos of high-wire act complexity stirring the juices of the most sedate into a bubbling rum punch. When the show is over and the band starts to play, rather than feeling that we couldn't possibly dance for at least an hour (lowly us after such an exhibition of talent), we take to the floor infused, as if by osmosis, with new found ability. Yes, we get it; five days of classes and all the milongas —we get it!

The band quits at midnight; it seems like they just started. We storm their gates for two encores, then we acquiesce because we know the DJ will play tangos all night. The floor is dense with dancers. I don't make it all the way around the floor even once in a song. But who cares?

Slowly an exodus begins. Couples say good-bye. Some just slip out. Maybe they live in Portland or San Francisco and can dance tomorrow night. Some, like myself, are voracious for all I can take in this last night; it will likely be months before I get to attend even a middle-sized milonga again. By two o'clock, nearly half of the four hundred plus people have left or are putting on their coats. A hundred people were still dancing, but there's noticeably more room again. In the next hour, most everyone else will have left and we entered an entirely new time — the all night milonga.

By three in the morning, the scene before me barely resembles what I joined a mere six hours before. Only sixty people remain — the gender split close to even. Gone is the buzz of background noise. The only sound is the music of tango. All but a handful of people dance every song. The few of us not dancing sit quietly on the sides and provide the audience for fifty people who aren't concerned with the eyes of others. Who is left at this late hour? Ages range from mid-twenties to mid-fifties. Six teachers remain. At the beginning of the evening, I could count myself in the upper-middle of dance skill, a solid intermediate dancer. Now I am at the bottom of the talent pool with one other guy, the rest of the leaders having years of greater proficiency to their credit. And the women are excellent dancers — every one of them. My ego is waving red flags to my brain; I've gone from being popular to the bottom of the heap.

I settle back and watch. Floor space is ample for all styles. Some take advantage of the room and perform dizzying combinations of difficult steps not very different from most of the exhibitions earlier in the evening. Two men in their twenties pair off for a wild display of testosterone-inspired acrobatic tango involving continuous fast turns and dangerous kicks, never missing. They exchange the lead and place the bar higher and higher to see just what is possible. Yet very few people are watching them.

Most of the couples are still dancing so tight against each other that I wonder how they could still twist and turn like they do. The couples barely relax their embrace between songs and keep dancing — twenty minutes? thirty minutes? The time clocks have all been turned off. They may be dancing with their spouses or with someone they've only known on the dance floor.

I venture to ask a woman to dance who hasn't danced in fifteen minutes. She's much better than I am, but is still gracious. I am even more struck by the emptiness of the floor from the perspective of dancing on it. Just three hours before one could barely move. Now, there is no place to hide. Certainly, no one watches me, the least talented of all the leaders on the floor, but everyone's aware of who is there. I dance four songs with my partner, while I sweat with the nervousness of a beginner that I haven't felt for over a year. Still, she seems genuinely grateful. I take my seat again.

The DJ is no longer constrained at this hour by the conservative conventions of prime-time when the producers of an event want only tangos by the classic orchestras with their consistent well-defined rhythms. He plays a Piazzolla set, the first great innovator of classic tango music, and then leaves the marked trail altogether. A set of tango music begins with all the angst and drama of a modern urban fable. Electronic synthesizers tell epic tragedies of a couple fighting for their lives and their love through the pounding of heartless mechanical devices. Grinding and screeching machinery seek to drown out the breath of the bandoneon. In one piece, the rhythm pounds like a driving piston, louder and louder, making even D'Arienzo look flexible. The dancing becomes ominous. I am spellbound by one couple in particular. The leader has set up a relentless mechanical meter in his steps, shoulders rotating slightly as if levers on a shaft. The follower, entirely up for the challenge, meshes like gears to his body from leg to cheek. They march their way down a pulsing assembly-line producing products of passion. Their eyes in a wide dream-state, fixed on the well-oiled moment of a device that purrs with the sweet hum of intimate precision. Such mastery of interpretation! I almost felt inappropriate staring. I wished I still had my video camera.

With the industrial-age machine banished at a safe distance once again, couples return to more traditional tango ecstasies. All is normal until one of the male teachers turns against the line of direction and swims upstream. At first, this wayward couple is ignored and passed by like a stalled car in the road. No one has appeared all that interested in anyone else not in their arms for hours. But he's intentionally breaking the cardinal rule of direction and must be dealt with. Annoyed glances turn to smiles of acknowledgment. Another couple joins the first couple's contrary direction. Soon half of the twenty remaining couples have reversed the consecrated flow of the river and chaos reigns until the end of the song when order is restored silently, just like the divergence itself began.

It's five o'clock and the remaining thirty-five people appear prepared to see the dawn together. I dance two sets with different partners, both superb dancers and quick to smooth-over a poor lead. Camaraderie and gratitude fill the room. You don't dance in this close and intimate way with someone and not care for them. Yet, as the sun comes up and dancing shoes are removed, the only people who leave together were couples before the week began. For all of the sensuality in tango, it has never appeared to me to be a social arrangement for meeting potential romantic partners. Is this only because I'm married and haven't been approached for that reason? I don't think so. Tango is a sacred space for men and women to love each other in all of our human frailty and splendor. Certainly many sexual encounters have been inspired by tango and a few marriage seeds have been sown in a milonga, but tango creates a greater possibility for adoring respect between all men and women than anything else I've ever heard of. Too bad it's so hard to learn; though doesn't all greatness require our full attention?

Six o'clock and the DJ announces two more dances, the last one being, of course, *La Cumparsita*. I watch the last seven couples still dancing while everyone else prepares for the outside and gives generous wishes to tango friends. The song ends and the dancers demand an encore! Another version of *La Cumparsita* is played (it's got to be the last song, after all). I leave alone, while the music is still playing—straining strings and squeezed bandoneons becoming fainter and fainter as I meet the quiet Portland Monday morning. Tango, its emotion and sensitivity, now pervades every day of my life, even when a day doesn't include dancing. I'll be back.

APPENDIX I: TANGO RESOURCES

Tango Camps

The camps and festivals listed below are ones we have attended ourselves or have enough details about from others that we can vouch for. Camps are not fixed in stone, however, so these are subject to change over time. You might get yourself on a mailing list for one that appeals to you.

Miami Tango Fantasy: Yearly in May (Memorial Day weekend), held at the Fountainbleau Hotel in Miami Beach. International atmosphere. Choose from a weekend or week packages. Lessons all day with the maestros, milonga with live music nightly. www.TangoFantasy.com

New York Tango Festival: Yearly in July, includes instructional programs and milongas in intimate, sophisticated venues. www.tangotours.com

Las Vegas: Yearly in September or October, a lively three day weekend in a hotel (returning after a hiatus in 2006). Classes daily with a mixture of American teachers and maestros. www.LasVegastango.com

Portland Tango Fest: Yearly in October with a mini fest over Valentine's weekend; a homegrown festival with Northwest feel and casual atmosphere. Most teachers are Americans with a few Argentine surprise guests. www.claydancestudio.com

Nora's Tango Week: Yearly in July at a hotel near Berkeley and San Francisco; choose from weekend or week packages; International atmosphere; classes all day with maestros, milongas nightly with live music. www.norastangoweek.com

Denver Tango: Yearly Labor Day and Memorial Day weekends; strictly milonguero close embrace style; full slate of American teachers, reasonable prices. www.tango.org

Fandango de Tango: Yearly in Austin Texas during Thanksgiving Week; full schedule of a variety of teachers. www.learn2dance.com

International Trips

Exotic Tango Vacations runs fascinating trips all over the world which include tango lessons with selected maestros. In a vacation mode, everyone seems to learn more easily. Contact Christina Johnson at www.beyondtango.com

Tango Cruises: We've heard good reports about cruises packaged by Cruises Plus; ask about "Tango at Sea," an annual cruise in October with excellent teachers and exotic destinations. www.cruisesplus.com

Selected U.S. Cities Tango Contacts

We can only mention a few here from among the contacts we ourselves have explored. Our best advice is to do a web search for: Your City or State+tango
Los Angeles: www.tangosplash.com
San Francisco: www.batango.com (This is a non profit association dedicated to promoting Argentine tango in the Bay Area. This is tango city U.S.A., where you can dance and/or take lessons every night.
Seattle: www.tangoing.com or www.claydancestudio.com
Portland: www.claydancestudio.com
New York City: NYC's tango magazine, ReporTango, reads like a menu for the impressive NYC tango scene (even though not always

proofread). It also lists updated tango contacts for the major cities in 20 states. www.reportango.com and www.nyctango.com
Hawaii: www.tangofire.net; email islatango@yahoo.com
The Argentine Tango Society: theargentinetangosociety@yahoo.com

Trips to Buenos Aires

Individuals and groups based in every major American city offer packaged trips that usually include airfare, accommodations, lessons, special outings and evening guides to the best milongas. BATango and NYCTango both list trips on their websites. A number of trips are run during two annual international festivals held in Buenos Aires: The World Tango Festival in October and the Congress of International Tango(CITA) in March. Reports are that these are exciting to attend, and the daily classes are superb, but the nightly milongas are simply too crowded to allow for real dancing. Nonetheless, Americans and Europeans keep coming.

Tango List-serves

If you would like to receive a constant stream of uncensored tango commentary, opinion, and fact, consider subscribing to either of the following. To subscribe, send email to listserve@mitva.mit.edu. In the message body, put the command
"subscribe TANGO-L (or TANGO-A) your full name"
Tango L is a discussion list-serve for any aspect of tango.
Tango A is an announcement list for upcoming tango events

Tango Clothes and Shoes

For glamorous dancing clothes visit www.tangoleva.com and www. dancedress.com

www.mrtangoshoes.com by Jorge Nel Girald of Dance Design is widely popular.

www.experienceshoes.com based in Seattle gets good reports

www.taratangoshoes.com represents the author's favorite tango shoes and well worth the price ($140-180). Men's shoes also available.

Another alternative is to go to Buenos Aires and arrange for custom-made shoes at one third the cost of factory-made shoes sold in this country and thus make your trip pay off in still another way.

Tango Movies, Instructional Videos, and CD's

These full length films are all available from most video stores or from "The Tango Catalogue," online at thetangocatalog.com.
Tango (directed by Carlos Saura)
The Tango Lesson (directed by Sally Potter)
Assassination Tango (directed by Robert Duvall)
Tango Bar
Tango Our Dance

Instructional videos are a great way to keep working on your tango between lessons and workshops. Since there are so many of these on the market, and more every year, it's best to ask a teacher for recommendations. We had good experiences with videos made by Daniel Trenner and by the team of Carolina Zokalsi and Diego di Falco.

Recommended CD's

An all round good source for CD's, videos and other tango products is "The Tango Catalogue" which comes both in hard copy and online at thetangocatalog.com. Also try thetangostore.com, abrazosbooks.com and tangocity.com.

Here below are some suggestions for building a danceable tango CD collection.

Carlos di Sarli y Su Orquesta Tipica, *"A La Gran Muneca"* (with singers)

Carlos di Sarli y Su Orquesta Tipica, Instrumental—in the *Tango Argentino* series

Osvaldo Pugliese—all titles

Anibal Troilo—*"Las Grandes Orquestas del Tango,"* two volumes

"The Tango Lesson" movie soundtrack

Sexteto Major, "Argentina"

Tango Federico, "A Dancemaster's Choice"

Hugo Diaz, *"Homenaje a Carlos Gardel"*

Hugo Diaz, *"Pero Yo Se"*

Tango No. 9, "All Them Cats in Recoleta"

Orquesta Color Tango, "The Story of Tango," volumes 1 and 2

"Assassination Tango," movie soundtrack

Caceres, *"Toca Tango"* (mostly Afro-influenced, milonga tempos)

Gotan Project, *"La Revancha del Tango"* (hybrid euro-techno style)

Dance Floor Etiquette

1. Don't get on the dance floor before you can reasonably navigate around the floor. Keep in mind that watching experienced dancers is at least as instructive as practicing, particularly in the early stages of learning.

2. Don't practice steps from class on the dance floor once a *milonga* has begun. Save practice for a *practica*. Move off the dance floor at a *milonga* to work out new steps.

3. Follow the line of dance, that is, in a counter-clockwise direction.

4. Do not lead or execute large or potentially injurious steps when the floor is crowded. In any case, master such steps off the dance floor first.

5. Don't correct your partner, simply go with the lead or follow as it is given. The only place acceptable for correcting is within the context of a lesson. Even then, it is more effective to call upon the instructor to help you both.

6. Don't apologize for a misstep. Everyone experiences them, whether as a leader or a follower. Expect missteps to happen. Learning to smooth over mistakes, yours and your partner's is part of the skills-set of tango. Getting to the place where a presumed misstep becomes an opportunity for something new is the mark of an advanced dancer.

7. Make eye contact with your partner between songs in a set (*tanda*). Thank her or him after the last dance. Feel free to say something complimentary.

APPENDIX II: BUENOS AIRES… IF YOU GO

EVERYONE WHO FALLS in love with tango dreams of eventually going to Buenos Aires, *El Corazon de Tango*, the mother country, so to speak, to dance and to make a pilgrimage. It isn't necessary, mind you, now that you can find tango teaching and milongas in so many cities closer to home. But if you have a desire to experience tango at its source, there are a number of options to choose from. You can travel independently and find your own way to tango clubs, or you can go independently but during a tango festival such as CITA where workshops are in ample supply and the streets are teeming with *tangueros*. Those who want the security of a guided group at any time of year can join one of the many excursions sponsored by dance instructors across the U.S. (see Appendix I)

Milongas of Buenos Aires

Tango venues in Buenos Aires are as varied as the restaurants; the dance clubs may all serve tango, but their "menus" and presentations differ vastly. The following list of Buenos Aires (BA) milongas is not even close to comprehensive. The clubs described herein only represent what I was able to experience during three weeks in November, 2003. Keep in mind that most of the clubs I attended only once – every venue has off nights. This summary represents maybe a fourth of the locations just within the *Distrito Federal* (greater Buenos Aires). Combine this stat with the fact that different organizers and DJs may sponsor alternate nights at the same venue creating a radically altered crowd and you can see that another person could have been in Buenos Aires the same weeks as I, danced every night, never crossed my path, and had very different experiences. Pick up a copy of *El Tangauta* and *El Firulete* which painstakingly list the location and promoter of every milonga and most of the classes for every night. The following synopses will, at least, give an idea of the range, directing you to where you might find the most enjoyment.

El Beso

Tuesday nights. A small, centrally located club with a single row of tables on three sides. Tastefully drab. The stylish hanging lamps are really two sizes of automobile air filters wired together – unused ones; too bad they couldn't be employed to take smoke out of the air of the club, though then they'd have to change them once a week (daily?). The twenty-five by thirty foot floor was packed until close to closing time. Lots of foreigners and Argentines dancing in courteous close embrace. Frequent partner exchanging. Intimate and *not* for the claustrophobic. They also have a Saturday night happening until six in the morning which I hear is well attended.

Castel – *Porteños y Bailarenes*

Also Tuesday nights—attracts the late-nighters (after 1 AM) leaving *El Beso* because it's only a block away. The *Castel* has two dance floors on either side of its "L" shape with the bar in the middle. It was very crowded both nights we were here. The back floor is assisted by two giant fans that send the smoke and heat flying out the front entrance; which is much appreciated except that when you dance by them they change the part of your hair and literally throw you off balance. Each night at about 2 AM they had a couple show-dance a few numbers. This was actually a good time to dance on the second floor and take advantage of the space. It was in this club that I encountered the two rudest dancers of the trip: one, an Argentine man who bulled his way *backwards* down the line of dance; and the second, a foreigner, who made fast sweeping turns with his pointed elbow extended to clear-out room for his partner's *boleos*. And me without my knife (it fell out in the taxi). Only came here twice because it was close.

Dandi

One of our favorites and only a hundred feet from our room in San Telmo. Wednesday's only. Run by a dynamic *Portena* standing all of 4'10", but well-rounded, who asks foreign men to dance with her if you frequent her club (we went three times). The *Dandi* is small, bright, and cheery. It has a very good wood floor of ample size with two big supporting poles to increase the level of difficulty or hide behind, as the case may be. Supports a regular cast of friendly Argentines and draws tourists as well. Actually has a non-smoking section, which means you have to ask for an ashtray (don't worry, there's plenty of them).

Confiteria La Ideal

Big deteriorating hall with restaurant below in the center of downtown. The waiters during the day are so old you're not sure they'll make it through the meal. Frequently boasts a live orchestra on Thursdays, which is when we were there. La Ideal also has several afternoon dances (ends before midnight). The atmosphere is grand, if you don't focus on details too clearly, which a lot of the senior clientele can no longer do anyway. The floor is giant, tile on wood and in better shape than the walls. The orchestra was great and played early (about midnight). When they returned to recorded music around 1 AM, the crowd thinned out fast. Both "The Tango Lesson" and "Evita" used this space for a movie-scene. Definitely merits at least one evening.

Salon El Pial – La Baldosa

Way out on the Northwest fringe of the city, but worth it (a whopping $4 cab ride). *El Pial* is a neighborhood club of mixed age *Porteños*—just a handful of foreigners. Large tile floor in a no frills meeting hall with great live music on Fridays, although the orchestra doesn't start until 2 AM and only plays forty-five minutes. People were exceedingly friendly, but mainly danced within their own groups. A lot of mediocre dancers, including a few youngsters having fun dancing open-style in the middle. Good pizza.

Lo De Celia

Tucked into the transvestite fringe of San Telmo (seen from the cab ride to and fro), *Lo De Celia* boasts many of the best old dancers on Sunday nights. Close embrace tango at its finest by a crowd that has been dancing for a very long time. Intimidating because nearly everyone is great, but they were still very welcoming. Take a table around the twenty-five foot square floor and watch for awhile. They make it look so deceptively easy. Swing and Latin sets are included on Sunday; some of the old guys and gals shake-out a mean merengue. On Monday, the crowd was way different, younger, and more foreigners; amazing the contrast on back-to-back nights.

Mi Club

Our one foray outside of the *Disticto Federal* for tango. We were invited to an open invitation birthday bash for a teacher of tango in this giant dance hall with five floors — three inside and two outside, though only one of the interior floors was being used. I felt welcome, but out of place; the moderate crowd all appeared to have lots of friends. I wanted a hundred more people, strangers to each other and all floors hopping. *Mi Club* looked like a budget (although large) seventies disco hall, but I saw it mentioned as a major club in the forties, though I suspect it has been remodeled. More effort than it was worth (a $6, 40 minute cab ride), but interesting.

La Catedral

I went from feeling like "one of the kids" at *Lo De Celia* to a parent at *La Catedral,* although there were about ten people older than I. The cab dropped me off at the appropriate corner and left. I walked around looking for the 4006 address, but that number didn't exist. No signs either about a club of any kind. Hardly even any lights. One young guy with long hair comes walking out of the darkness holding a singe rose in front of his face. I ask if he knows of a tango club real close to here. "*La Catedral,* behind those doors. You're welcome." I approach the black unmarked double doors and push. It creaks open and I see a decaying stairway ascending in a milky light. I take a few steps inside and then, the music. Two flights up in a building that would be closed to the public in the States is a tango club unlike anything I've ever heard of. Thirty foot walls with a patched tin roof keep out most of the rain. Large wild modern paintings adorn the walls of the otherwise techno-grunge décor. A dozen old pieces of furniture and cushions act as couches covered with sprawled-out, dressed-down youth. Another ten tables with mismatched chairs give one a foot-hold on normal. I changed shoes on a couch more duct-tape than vinyl, abandoned because of a drip directly above and stashed my stuff near an abyss with a wired-off spiral staircase that descended into garbage. The floor is wood with the level of cobblestones. Most of the time, the music is the same as everywhere else at milongas around the world. Then they played a "Narco Tango" set and changed that. The quality of dancing was pretty good, though a few beginners blundered along. Perhaps a third were foreigners. The floor is only about twenty by twenty (it undulates, or was there something in my *agua sin gas?*), but it's rarely too full. They still mainly dance close embrace, which surprised me — I expected more showy open style. At 2 AM a long white cloth was stretched to contain a slideshow of Diane Arbus-like street scenes while Spanish, English, and German poetry droned. Next, they emptied bags of dry garbage on the dance floor and picked it up with packaging tape in snowballing bundles. Then they spread a ten by fifteen plastic sheet on the floor and pulled five (two women, three men) previously arranged members from the audience (I hope), stripped them naked, laid them on the plastic, poured mud on them, and mopped them down. This not being enough, they painted them multi-colors with their hands. For the finale, they threw a tarp over them and all five living canvases and their three painters screamed and tumbled together. Show's over. Anyone for a Pugliese set? The floor was crowded — obviously just the right kind of inspiration for the group. Intriguing fact: *La Catedral* had the best sound system and volume setting combination of all the clubs – most places being too loud, sometimes painfully, especially when you dance by the speakers. The kids had it right.

Niño Bien

Niño Bien is one of the most upscale major venues (*La Catedral* not being on the scale). It has the grandness of *La Ideal* without the decay. Vaulted ceilings capturing the smoke. Big enough for three rows of tables all the way around an eighty-by-twenty dance floor which was still full by the end of the second song of each *tanda*. Lots of great dancers. We saw Eduardo and Gloria of "Forever Tango" fame, but they weren't dancing, at least not by when we left close to 3 AM. This was the most elegant club we went to.

Sunderland Club

On Saturdays only, they lift the basketball apparatus back against the walls of the gymnasium and invent the Sunderland Club. Most of the bleachers are pulled back to make room for a large number of tables. The floor is, oddly enough, tile (I would hate to play basketball on it) and a forty-by-forty square. The sound is loud and tinny, since there isn't a soft surface in the room other than the humans. Very friendly big group of dancers, though mostly Argentines. Four giant propeller fans (think WWII fighter planes) "grace" the corners of the gym about twenty feet high; when they engage them, the smoke roars out of the clerestory windows and it's hard to hear the music. They don't leave them on long. Very mixed age group. Great dancers.

Torquato Tasso

Great live music every Friday, Saturday, and Sunday, but this club on the Sunday I went was more of a listening venue than dance joint. Yes, they have a tiny ten-by-fifteen floor, but hardly anyone danced when the band of four guitars and singer were performing (they were very good). When the recorded music began, the floor filled instantly to way more than comfortable. Some inconsiderates still tried big open work, bumping into people with regularity. Nobody got upset though. Reminded me of taxi rides on the twenty-lane Avenida de Julio Boulevard during rush hour; there are no apparent rules except try to miss everyone and no one gets tweaked. I still had enthusiastic dancers and good conversations, but I doubt that I'll go back.

Salon Canning

This is one of the six places you can dance on a Monday night (there are twenty on Saturday) and it turned out to be my favorite venue period. We paid twice what we paid to get in anywhere else (about $4). The square, high ceiling room is bright and clean; large interesting art on the walls and a beautiful thirty-by-thirty wood floor. At least half in

attendance were foreigners, but the dancing caliber was still high. At one o'clock a guitar and bandoneon played for dancing—marvelous. They played twenty minutes, took an hour break, and played another set (I would have preferred hour sets and twenty minute breaks, right?). A great place to both dance and meet people.

Centro Armenio "La Viruta"

The "Big Saturday Dance" I'd been anxious to see was too crowded to be simpatico, but too Buenos Aires to be unfriendly. It was just too much. The large floor was packed, yet they added tables to the floor space for extra seating room; something's wrong with this picture. Too many people milling all about to feel relaxed. The low ceiling in this barren meeting hall just added to the din and repressive air. Maybe it would be better on a Wednesday or Friday. Someone told me it was best from 4 to 6 in the morning. A singer and keyboard appeared on the floor for a half-hour show. At 3 AM the crowd was still at maximum and we left to walk the two blocks to Salon Canning to catch the last hour there. There were maybe fifteen older Argentines fanning a dying flame of what had been my favorite place only the last Monday. Why couldn't a hundred people from *Centro Armenio* (out of the 400+) join us here? It was only a five minute walk. Just one of the mysteries of the Buenos Aires tango scene.

Dance Etiquette in Buenos Aires

Buenos Aires has a tightly followed code for the pre-dance, known as the *cabeceo*. If you don't understand it, you will likely be, as a man, surprised at the number of rejections from women at your invitation to dance, or, as a woman, terribly disappointed that no one asked you to dance. Even foreigners who don't usually live by the Buenos Aires code in their homeland will usually be aware of it in BA and follow it strictly. Know the etiquette for both men and women.

First, the men. In the United States, men approach a woman they want to dance with, get her attention with a touch on the shoulder or by suddenly standing in her view, and ask her to dance; the vast majority of the time the woman says yes. In BA, eye contact accompanied by an indication of acceptance *must preface the verbal*

invitation. In fact, many times, this *is* the invitation followed by the man and woman making their way towards each other and stepping into dance position. After the first dance, they usually exchange names and a few words about where they're from. Making quick eye contact from a few feet away is not enough; there must be a nod of the head towards the dance floor or an extended meeting of the eyes, usually with the raising of eyebrows or widening of the eyes. This is your answer. Make your way over to her, if she wasn't standing she will likely have stood up by the time you arrive. I usually ask verbally to make sure, but if they've already walked out onto the dance floor, further words are unneeded and doesn't sound like a voice of confidence, the appearance of confidence being an important trait to cultivate.

Only a woman who looks like she wants to dance will get asked. Talking with your friend, just watching the dancers, or any other avoidance of eye contact will keep you in your seat or standing by the wall. Also, don't sit too affectionately close to a man you came with; this will be seen as a sign of disinterest in dancing with anyone else. Yes, you might get the occasional foreigner who isn't concerned about protocol, especially if there is a shortage of women. If you come as a couple, dance together showing off your best form and technique, nothing flashy. Men—don't try to impress anyone (you won't) with fancy steps. A lot of Argentines, men and women, won't dance with a foreigner until they know your skill level. Again, it's a grasp of the basics that matters, not that back *sacada* that wows your friends back home. Such stage tango moves might result in no eye contact with any Argentine all night.

Women, if you want to dance a lot, especially with Argentines, follow these guidelines. Keep your head up and your eyes moving. If where you are sitting doesn't afford easy sight lines to prospective partners, stand up and walk around. When you make eye contact, don't panic. If for whatever reason you don't want to dance with this man, just look away, continuing your search; very few men will think this was acceptance. If you want to try a dance with this man, hold the eye contact. If he looks away, don't let it dent you; he might just have been looking for someone he knows or be such a discriminate

jerk you wouldn't want him anyway. Keep your own search going. When his eyes stay with yours, you've got one on the line. Raise your eyes to inquire silently "Shall we dance?" If he nods to the floor or starts your way, you've done it—no backing out now. If you lose eye contact, you may wait until he's close before standing up, but if he continues looking at you, be gracious and meet him part way. Never raise eyebrows, nod, and then say no; Argentines especially would find this insulting, possibly requiring a stiff drink after a taxi ride to a different club.

Pitfalls. Occasionally, someone is making eye-contact with a person behind you; you nod, get up, only to realize that the person you thought was looking at you heads right past you to another person. Just keep walking to the bar or bathroom like that's what you intended all along. This can happen to both men and women.

Another less than ideal scenario happened to me at Lo de Celia where no one met my eyes for a long time. I wandered the perimeter trying to catch any woman's gaze, but received less attention than Gardel's picture on the wall. I just had to be patient; finally one woman took a chance and the night's dancing began. A woman who sits up straight, scanning the crowd for a partner, and doesn't get invited to dance has the worst of ego-testing to endure.

One club where these rules were lax was *La Catedral* (not surprised?). For one thing, it was too dark to make eye-contact across the room. The younger crowd, packed with foreigners didn't appear to hold protocol high on their priority list. It was here that I danced with a woman still in her twenties that labeled herself a *milonguera* (tangos most nights every week, has mastered the dance, and really has no other life worth mentioning) before beginning the critique of my dancing. She told me that my right arm shouldn't have contact anywhere on her, not even at her side where most teachers recommend; that my arm should be like a ring that she is free to dance within (it was a good thing she was thin). "What about protecting you from bumping into others," I asked. "There is no need for that," she countered, "a *milonguera* can sense where everyone is behind her without seeing them." I was hoping to get to test her claim, but she walked off.

References Cited

Holland, Bernard. "Passion for Tango West Coast and East." *NYTimes.com*, March 3, 2004

Miller, Susana. Interview in *ReporTango*, The New York Tango Magazine #22, September, 2002

Pellicoro, Paul. *Paul Pellicoro on Tango*. Barricade Books Inc. 2002

Savigliano, Marta. *Tango and the Political Economy of Passion*. Boulder, Westview Press, 1995.

Siegmann, Johanna. *The Tao of Tango*. Trafford Publishing, 2003

Suarez, Carlos. El Jazz, the Tango," Liner notes from CD *All them cats in Recoleta* by Tango No. 9

Taylor, Juliet. "Addiction," *Voz del Tango*, volume 6, number 4, 2001

Taylor, Juliet. *Paper Tangos*, Duke University Press, 1999

Author

Biographies

Irene D. Thomas, Ph.D. made a career in academia and educational publishing and later found a midlife hobby in ballroom dancing. Like others before them, though, once she and her husband discovered Argentine Tango, they never looked back. Today they introduce others to the joys of tango and whenever possible follow the tango trail around the country. This book grew out of a passion to tell the story of what happens to Americans when they take on this fascinating and provocative dance form—and the culture that goes with it. Her essays about tango, mostly drawing upon her own experience, provide a contextual background for her friend Larry Sawyer's tango stories. Together they may have created a new genre, combining fiction and non-fiction in an original format.

She lives with her husband on the Mendocino Coast of Northern California.

Larry Sawyer pursued a working life of Land-Use Planning and the rather dry writing of Environmental Impact Reports before letting it go in favor of romance and adventure on the Mendocino Coast. After learning all of the commonly found partner dances in the U.S., he and his wife found Argentine tango in the late nineties. Soon after, all dance classes they took were tango. Travel within the States or abroad now includes a search for tango in the local area. Obsession with fulfillment is a wonderful thing, especially if all you lose along the way is your foxtrot. His stories represent a return to an earlier passion for writing fiction.

Larry also lives with his wife, Harriet, in Albion on the Mendocino Coast.

ISBN 1-41206413-9

9 781412 064132